Bernard Berenson

The Venetian painters of the renaissance, with an index to their works

Third Edition

Bernard Berenson

The Venetian painters of the renaissance, with an index to their works
Third Edition

ISBN/EAN: 9783337663810

Printed in Europe, USA, Canada, Australia, Japan

Cover: Foto ©ninafisch / pixelio.de

More available books at **www.hansebooks.com**

THE VENETIAN PAINTERS

OF

THE RENAISSANCE

WITH AN INDEX TO THEIR WORKS

BY

BERNHARD BERENSON

AUTHOR OF "FLORENTINE PAINTERS OF THE RENAISSANCE,"
"CENTRAL ITALIAN PAINTERS OF THE RENAISSANCE"

THIRD EDITION

G. P. PUTNAM'S SONS
NEW YORK AND LONDON
The Knickerbocker Press

COPYRIGHT, 1894
BY
G. P. PUTNAM'S SONS

Entered at Stationers' Hall, London.
BY G. P. PUTNAM'S SONS

NOTE TO THIRD EDITION.

IN this edition changes have been made in the numbering of the Venice and Vienna Galleries, as well as of some minor collections, to correspond to recent rehanging. Many other alterations have been required by the breaking up of private collections. In several instances it has been impossible to trace pictures to their new homes, and of such the more important remain under the names of their former owners. To the lists of painters have been added Beccaruzzi, Caprioli, Polidoro Lanzani, Rocco Marconi, Andrea Schiavone, and Girolamo da Treviso, artists important enough to be missed, but of merit so unequal that only their more interesting works are here given. But the bulk of new additions, amounting to a third as much again as was comprised in the last edition, is of pictures in the various provincial galleries and private collections of Great Britain, France, and Germany.

The author takes great pleasure in acknowledging his indebtedness to Mr. Herbert F. Cook for invaluable aid in visiting some of the almost numberless British collections.

NOTE TO THE SECOND EDITION.

THE indices of this second edition have been carefully revised, and a considerable number of additions have been made to the lists.

The author begs once more to call attention to the fact that, with one or two exceptions, *he has mentioned no pictures that he has not seen.* The lists are the result, not of compilation, but of first-hand acquaintance with the works of art.

PREFACE.

THE following essay owes its origin to the author's belief that Venetian painting is the most complete expression in art of the Italian Renaissance. The Renaissance is even more important typically than historically. Historically it may be looked upon as an age of glory or of shame according to the different views entertained of European events during the past five centuries. But typically it stands for youth, and youth alone—for intellectual curiosity and energy grasping at the whole of life as material which it hopes to mould to any shape.

Every generation has an innate sympathy with some epoch of the past wherein it seems to find itself foreshadowed. Science has of late revealed and given much, but its revelation and gifts are as nothing to the promise it holds out of constant acquisition and perpetual growth, of everlasting youth. We ourselves, because of our faith in science and the power of work, are instinctively in sympathy with the Renaissance. Our problems do not seem so easy to solve, our tasks are more difficult because our vision is wider, but the spirit which animates us was anticipated by the spirit of the Renaissance, and more than anticipated. That spirit seems like the small rough model after which ours is being fashioned.

Italian painting interests many of us more than the painting of any other school not because of its essential superiority, but because it expressed the Renaissance; and Venetian painting is interesting above all because it was at Venice alone that this expression attained perfection. Elsewhere, particularly in Florence, it died away before it found complete utterance.

In order to keep the main idea clearly before the mind of the reader, to show him how the Renaissance reveals itself in Venetian painting, the introduction of anything not strictly relevant to the subject has been avoided. The salient points once perceived and connected with the more important painters, the reader will find no difficulty in seeing the proper place of any given work by a great master, or the relative importance of those second- and third-rate painters of whom no special mention has been made because they are comprised within what has been said about the greater artists.

But happily art is too great and too vital a subject to be crowded into any single formula; and a formula that would, without distorting our entire view of Italian art in the fifteenth century, do full justice to such a painter as Carlo Crivelli, does not exist. He takes rank with the most genuine artists of all times and countries, and does not weary even when "great masters" grow tedious. He expresses with the freedom and spirit of Japanese design a piety as wild and tender as Jacopo da Todi's, a sweetness of emotion as sincere and dainty as of a Virgin and Child carved in ivory by a French craftsman of the fourteenth century. The mystic beauty of Simone Martini, the agonized compassion of the young Bellini, are embodied by Crivelli in forms which have the strength of line and the metallic lustre of old Satsuma or lacquer, and which are no less tempting to the touch. Crivelli must be treated by himself and as the product of stationary, if not reactionary, conditions. Having lived most of his life far away from the main currents of culture, in a province where St. Bernardino had been spending his last energies in the endeavour to call the world back to the ideals of an infantile civilisation, Crivelli does not belong to a movement of constant progress, and therefore is not within the scope of this work.

To make the essay useful as a handbook to Venetian painting, lists have been appended of the works, in and out of Italy, by the principal Venetian masters. These lists do not pretend to absolute completeness. Only such private collections have been mentioned as are well known and accessible to students, although in the case of very rare painters all of their known works are given, and even such as are of doubtful authenticity are alluded to. The author has seen and carefully considered all the pictures he mentions, except one or two at St. Petersburg, which are, however, well known from the photographs of MM. Braun & Cie. The attributions are based on the results of the most recent research. Even such painstaking critics of some years ago as Messrs. Crowe and Cavalcaselle laboured under terrible disadvantages, because most of their work was done at a time when travelling was much slower than it has now become, and when photography was not sufficiently perfected to be of great service. Rapid transit and isochromatic photography are beginning to enable the student to make of connoisseurship something like an exact science. To a certain extent, therefore, Messrs. Crowe and Cavalcaselle have been superseded, and to a great degree supplemented by the various writings of Morelli, Richter, Frizzoni, and others. The author takes pleasure in acknowledging his indebtedness to the first systematic writers on Italian painting no less than to the perfectors of the new critical method, now adopted by nearly all serious students of Italian art. To the founder of the new criticism, the late Giovanni Morelli, and to his able successor, Dr. Gustavo Frizzoni, the author feels bound to ascribe many of his attributions, although a number are based on independent research, and for these he alone is responsible. Special thanks are due to a dear friend, Enrico Costa, for placing his notes of a recent visit to Madrid at the author's disposal. They have been used, with a confidence warranted by Signor Costa's unrivalled connoisseurship, to supplement the author's own notes, taken some years ago.

Having noted the dependence of scientific art study upon isochromatic photography, the author is happy to take this opportunity of expressing his gratitude to such able photographers as Löwy of Vienna, Tamme of Dresden, Marcozzi of Milan, Alinari Bros. of Florence, and Dominic Anderson of Rome, all of whom have devoted themselves with special zeal to the paintings of the Venetian masters. The author is peculiarly indebted to Signor Anderson for having materially assisted his studies by photographing many pictures which at present have a scientific rather than a popular interest.

The frontispiece is a reproduction of Giorgione's "Shepherd" at Hampton Court, a picture which perhaps better than any other expresses the Renaissance at the most fascinating point of its course. The author is indebted to Mr. Sidney Colvin for permission to make use of a photograph taken at his order.

CONTENTS.

		PAGE
THE VENETIAN PAINTERS OF THE RENAISSANCE		1
I.	VALUE OF VENETIAN ART	1
II.	THE CHURCH AND PAINTING	2
III.	THE RENAISSANCE	5
IV.	PAINTING AND THE RENAISSANCE	12
V.	PAGEANT PICTURES	17
VI.	PAINTING AND THE CONFRATERNITIES	22
VII.	EASEL PICTURES AND GIORGIONE	26
VIII.	THE GIORGIONESQUE SPIRIT	31
IX.	THE PORTRAIT	32
X.	THE YOUNG TITIAN	38
XI.	APPARENT FAILURE OF THE RENAISSANCE	41
XII.	LOTTO	43
XIII.	THE LATE RENAISSANCE AND TITIAN	44
XIV.	HUMANITY AND THE RENAISSANCE	48
XV.	SEBASTIANO DEL PIOMBO	49
XVI.	TINTORETTO	51

CONTENTS.

		PAGE
XVII.	Value of Minor Episodes in Art	56
XVIII.	Tintoretto's Portraits	59
XIX.	Venetian Art and the Provinces	60
XX.	Paul Veronese	62
XXI.	Bassano, Genre, and Landscape	64
XXII.	The Venetians and Velasquez	70
XXIII.	Decline of Venetian Art	71
XXIV.	Longhi	72
XXV.	Canaletto and Guardi	74
XXVI.	Tiepolo	75
XXVII.	Influence of Venetian Art	77

INDEX TO THE WORKS OF THE PRINCIPAL VENETIAN PAINTERS 79

INDEX OF PLACES 131

THE VENETIAN PAINTERS OF
THE RENAISSANCE.

THE VENETIAN PAINTERS OF THE RENAISSANCE

I. Value of Venetian Art.—Among the Italian schools of painting the Venetian has, for the majority of art-loving people, the strongest and most enduring attraction. In the course of the present brief account of the life of that school we shall perhaps discover some of the causes of our peculiar delight and interest in the Venetian painters, as we come to realise what tendencies of the human spirit their art embodied, and of what great consequence their example has been to the whole of European painting for the last three centuries.

The Venetians as a school were from the first endowed with exquisite tact in their use of colour. Seldom cold and rarely too warm, their colouring never seems an afterthought, as in many of the Florentine painters, nor is it always suggesting paint, as in some of the Veronese masters. When the eye has grown accustomed to make allowance for the darkening caused by time, for the dirt that lies in layers on so many pictures, and for unsuccessful attempts at restoration, the better Venetian paintings present such harmony of intention and execution as distinguishes the highest achievements of genuine poets. Their mastery over colour is the first thing that attracts most people to the painters of Venice. Their colouring not only gives direct pleasure to the eye, but acts like music upon the moods, stimulating thought and memory in much the same way as a work by a great composer.

II. **The Church and Painting.**—The Church from the first took account of the influence of colour as well as of music upon the emotions. From the earliest times it employed mosaic and painting to enforce its dogmas and relate its legends, not merely because this was the only means of reaching people who could neither read nor write, but also because it instructed them in a way which, far from leading to critical enquiry, was peculiarly capable of being used as an indirect stimulus to moods of devotion and contrition. Next to the finest mosaics of the first centuries, the early works of Giovanni Bellini, the greatest Venetian master of the fifteenth century, best fulfil this religious intention. Painting had in his life-time reached a point where the difficulties of technique no longer stood in the way of the expression of profound emotion. No one can look at Bellini's pictures of the Dead Christ upheld by the Virgin or angels without being put into a mood of deep contrition, nor at his earlier Madonnas without a thrill of awe and reverence. And Giovanni Bellini does not stand alone. His contemporaries, Gentile Bellini, the Vivarini, Crivelli, and Cima da Conegliano all began by painting in the same spirit, and produced almost the same effect.

The Church, however, thus having educated people to understand painting as a language and to look to it for the expression of their sincerest feelings, could not hope to keep it always confined to the channel of religious emotion. People began to feel the need of painting as something that entered into their every-day lives almost as much as we nowadays feel the need of the newspaper; nor was this unnatural, considering that, until the invention of printing, painting was the only way, apart from direct speech, of conveying ideas to the masses. At about the time when Bellini and his contemporaries were attaining maturity, the Renaissance had ceased to be a movement carried on by scholars and poets alone. It had become sufficiently widespread to seek popular as well as literary utterance, and thus, toward the end of the fifteenth century, it naturally turned to painting, a vehicle of expression which the Church, after a thousand years of use, had made familiar and beloved.

To understand the Renaissance at the time when its spirit began to find complete embodiment in painting, a brief survey of the movement of thought in Italy during its earlier period is necessary, because only when that movement had reached a certain point did painting come to be its most natural medium of expression.

III. The Renaissance. — The thousand years that elapsed between the triumph of Christianity and the middle of the fourteenth century have been not inaptly compared to the first fifteen or sixteen years in the life of the individual. Whether full of sorrows or joys, of storms or peace, these early years are chiefly characterised by tutelage and unconsciousness of personality. But toward the end of the fourteenth century something happened in Europe that happens in the lives of all gifted individuals. There was an awakening to the sense of personality. Although it was felt to a greater or less degree everywhere, Italy felt the awakening earlier than the rest of Europe, and felt it far more strongly. Its first manifestation was a boundless and insatiable curiosity, urging people to find out all they could about the world and about man. They turned eagerly to the study of classic literature and ancient monuments, because these gave the key to what seemed an immense storehouse of forgotten knowledge; they were in fact led to antiquity by the same impulse which, a little later, brought about the invention of the printing-press and the discovery of America.

The first consequence of a return to classical literature was the worship of human greatness. Roman literature, which the Italians naturally mastered much earlier than Greek, dealt chiefly with politics and war, seeming to give an altogether disproportionate place to the individual, because it treated only of such individuals as were concerned in great events. It is but a step from realising the greatness of an event to believing that the persons concerned in it were equally great, and this belief, fostered by the somewhat rhetorical literature of Rome, met the new consciousness of personality more than half way, and led to that unlimited admiration for human genius and achievement which was so prominent a feature of the early Renaissance. The two tendencies reacted upon each other. Roman literature stimulated the admiration for genius, and this admiration in turn reinforced the interest in that period of the world's history when genius was supposed to be the rule rather than the exception; that is to say, it reinforced the interest in antiquity.

The spirit of discovery, the never satisfied curiosity of this time, led to the study of ancient art as well as of ancient literature, and the love of antiquity led to the imitation of its buildings and statues as well as of its books and poems. Until comparatively recent times scarcely any ancient paintings were found, although buildings and statues were everywhere to be seen, the moment anyone seriously thought of looking at them. The result was that while the architecture and sculpture of the Renaissance were directly and strongly influenced by antiquity, painting felt its influence only in so far as the study of antiquity, in the other arts had conduced to better draughtsmanship and purer taste. The spirit of discovery could thus show itself only indirectly in painting,—only in so far as it led painters to the gradual perfection of the technical means of their craft.

Unlimited admiration for genius and wonder that the personalities of antiquity should have survived with their great names in no way diminished, soon had two consequences. One was love of glory, and the other the patronage of those arts which were supposed to hand down a glorious name undiminished to posterity. The glory of old Rome had come down through poets and historians, architects and sculptors, and the Italians, feeling that the same means might be used to hand down the achievements of their own time to as distant a posterity, made a new religion of glory, with poets and artists for the priests. At first the new priesthood was confined almost entirely to writers, but in little more than a generation architects and sculptors began to have their part. The passion for building is in itself one of the most instinctive, and a man's name and armorial bearings, tastefully but prominently displayed upon a church or palace, were as likely, it was felt, to hand him down to posterity as the praise of poets or historians. It was the passion for glory, in reality, rather than any love of beauty, that gave the first impulse to the patronage of the arts in the Renaissance. Beauty was the concern of the artists, although no doubt their patrons were well aware that the more impressive a building was, the more beautiful a monument, the more likely was it to be admired, and the more likely were their names to reach posterity. Their instincts did not mislead them, for where their real achievements would have tempted only the specialist or antiquarian into a study of their career, the buildings and monuments put up by them—by such princes as Sigismondo Malatesta, Frederick of Urbino, or Alfonzo of Naples,—have made the whole intelligent public believe that they were really as great as they wished posterity to believe them.

As painting had done nothing whatever to transmit the glory of the great Romans, the earlier generations of the Renaissance expected nothing from it, and did not give it that patronage which the Church, for its own purposes, continued to hold out to it. The Renaissance began to make especial use of painting only when its own spirit had spread very widely, and when the love of knowledge, of power, and of glory had ceased to be the only recognised passions, and when, following the lead of the Church, people began to turn to painting for the expression of deep emotion.

The new religion, as I have called the love of glory, is in its very essence a thing of this world, founded as it is on human esteem. The boundless curiosity of the Renaissance led back inevitably to an interest in life and to an acceptance of things for what they were,—for their intrinsic quality. The moment people stopped looking fixedly toward heaven their eyes fell upon the earth, and they began to see much on its surface that was pleasant. Their own faces and figures must have struck them as surprisingly interesting, and, considering how little St. Bernard and other mediæval saints and doctors had led them to expect, singularly beautiful. A new feeling arose that mere living was a big part of life, and with it came a new passion, the passion for beauty, for grace, and for comeliness.

It has already been suggested that the Renaissance was a period in the history of modern Europe comparable to youth in the life of the individual. It had all youth's love of finery and of play. The more people were imbued with the new spirit, the more they loved pageants. The pageant was an outlet for many of the dominant passions of the time, for there a man could display all the finery he pleased, satisfy his love of antiquity by masquerading as Cæsar or Hannibal, his love of knowledge by finding out how the Romans dressed and rode in triumph, his love of glory by the display of wealth and skill in the management of the ceremony, and, above all, his love of feeling himself alive. Solemn writers have not disdained to describe to the minutest details many of the pageants which they witnessed.

We have seen that the earlier elements of the Renaissance, the passion for knowledge and glory, were not of the kind to give a new impulse to painting. Nor was the passion for antiquity at all so direct an inspiration to that art as it was to architecture and sculpture. The love of glory had, it is true, led such as could not afford to put up monumental buildings, to decorate chapels with frescoes in which their portraits were timidly introduced. But it was only when the Renaissance had attained to a full consciousness of its interest in life and enjoyment of the world that it naturally turned, and indeed was forced to turn, to painting; for it is obvious that painting is peculiarly fitted for rendering the appearances of things with a glow of light and richness of colour that correspond to and express warm human emotions.

IV. Painting and the Renaissance. —

When it once reached the point where its view of the world naturally sought expression in painting, as religious ideas had done before, the Renaissance found in Venice clearer utterance than elsewhere, and it is perhaps this fact which makes the most abiding interest of Venetian painting. It is at this point that we shall take it up.

The growing delight in life with the consequent love of health, beauty, and joy were felt more powerfully in Venice than anywhere else in Italy. The explanation of this may be found in the character of the Venetian government which was such that it gave little room for the satisfaction of the passion for personal glory, and kept its citizens so busy in duties of state that they had small leisure for learning. Some of the chief passions of the Renaissance thus finding no outlet in Venice, the other passions insisted all the more on being satisfied. Venice, moreover, was the only state in Italy which was enjoying, and for many generations had been enjoying, internal peace. This gave the Venetians a love of comfort, of ease, and of splendour, a refinement of manner, and humaneness of feeling, which made them the first really modern people in Europe. Since there was little room for personal glory in Venice, the perpetuators of glory, the Humanists, found at first scant encouragement there, and the Venetians were saved from that absorption in archæology and pure science which overwhelmed Florence at an early date. This was not necessarily an advantage in itself, but it happened to suit Venice, where the conditions of life had for some time been such as to build up a love of beautiful things. As it was, the feeling for beauty was not hindered in its natural development. Archæology would have tried to submit it to the good taste of the past, a proceeding which rarely promotes good taste in the present. Too much archæology and too much science might have ended in making Venetian art academic, instead of letting it become what it did, the product of a natural ripening of interest in life and love of pleasure. In Florence, it is true, painting had developed almost simultaneously with the other arts, and it may be due to this very cause that the Florentine painters never quite realised what a different task from the architect's and sculptor's was theirs. At the time, therefore, when the Renaissance was beginning to find its best expression in painting, the Florentines were already too much attached to classical ideals of form and composition, in other words, too academic, to give embodiment to the throbbing feeling for life and pleasure.

Thus it came to pass that in the Venetian pictures of the end of the fifteenth century we find neither the contrition nor the devotion of those earlier years when the Church alone employed painting as the interpreter of emotion, nor the learning which characterised the Florentines. The Venetian masters of this time, although nominally continuing to paint the Madonna and saints, were in reality painting handsome, healthy, sane people like themselves, people who wore their splendid robes with dignity, who found life worth the mere living and sought no metaphysical basis for it. In short, the Venetian pictures of the last decade of the century seemed intended not for devotion, as they had been, nor for admiration, as they then were in Florence, but for enjoyment.

The Church itself, as has been said, had educated its children to understand painting as a language. Now that the passions men dared to avow were no longer connected with happiness in some future state only, but mainly with life in the present, painting was expected to give voice to these more human aspirations and to desert the outgrown ideals of the Church. In Florence, the painters seemed unable or unwilling to make their art really popular. Nor was it so necessary there, for Poliziano, Pulci, and Lorenzo dei Medici supplied the need of self-expression by addressing the Florentines in the language which their early enthusiasm for antiquity and their natural gifts had made them understand better than any other—the language of poetry. In Venice alone painting remained what it had been all over Italy in earlier times, the common tongue of the whole mass of the people. Venetian artists thus had the strongest inducements to perfect the processes which painters must employ to make pictures look real to their own generation; and their generation had an altogether firmer hold on reality than any that had been known since the triumph of Christianity. Here again the comparison of the Renaissance to youth must be borne in mind. The grasp that youth has on reality is not to be compared to that brought by age, and we must not expect to find in the Renaissance a passion for an acquaintance with things as they are such as we ourselves have; but still its grasp of facts was far firmer than that of the Middle Ages.

Painting, in accommodating itself to the new ideas, found that it could not attain to satisfactory representation merely by form and colour, but that it required light and shadow and effects of space. Indeed, venial faults of drawing are perhaps the least disturbing, while faults of perspective, of spacing, and of colour completely spoil a picture for people who have an every-day acquaintance with painting such as the Venetians had. We find the Venetian painters, therefore, more and more intent upon giving the space they paint its real depth, upon giving solid objects the full effect of the round, upon keeping the different parts of a figure within the same plane, and upon compelling things to hold their proper places one behind the other. As early as the beginning of the sixteenth century a few of the greater Venetian painters had succeeded in making distant objects less and less distinct, as well as smaller and smaller, and had succeeded also in giving some appearance of reality to the atmosphere. These are a few of the special problems of painting, as distinct from sculpture for instance, and they are problems which, among the Italians, only the Venetians and the painters closely connected with them solved with any success.

V. Pageant Pictures.—The painters of the end of the fifteenth century who met with the greatest success in solving these problems were Giovanni and Gentile Bellini, Cima da Conegliano, and Carpaccio, and we find each of them enjoyable to the degree that he was in touch with the life of his day. I have already spoken of pageants and of how characteristic they were of the Renaissance, forming as they did a sort of safety-valve for its chief passions. Venice, too, knew the love of glory, and the passion was perhaps only the more intense because it was all dedicated to the State. There was nothing the Venetians would not do to add to its greatness, glory, and splendour. It was this which led them to make of the city itself that wondrous monument to the love and awe they felt for their Republic, which still rouses more admiration and gives more pleasure than any other one achievement of the art-impulse in man. They were not content to make their city the most beautiful in the world; they performed ceremonies in its honour partaking of all the solemnity of religious rites. Processions and pageants by land and by sea, free from that gross element of improvisation which characterised them elsewhere in Italy, formed no less a part of the functions of the Venetian State than the High Mass in the Catholic

Church. Such a function, with Doge and Senators arrayed in gorgeous costumes no less prescribed than the raiments of ecclesiastics, in the midst of the fairy-like architecture of the Piazza or canals, was the event most eagerly looked forward to, and the one that gave most satisfaction to the Venetian's love of his State, and to his love of splendour, beauty, and gaiety. He would have had them every day if it were possible, and, to make up for their rarity, he loved to have representations of them. So most Venetian pictures of the beginning of the sixteenth century tended to take the form of magnificent processions, if they did not actually represent them. They are processions in the Piazza, as in Gentile Bellini's "Corpus Christi" picture, or on the water, as in Carpaccio's picture where St. Ursula leaves her home; or they represent what was a gorgeous but common sight in Venice, the reception or dismissal of ambassadors, as in several pictures of Carpaccio's St. Ursula series; or they show simply a collection of splendidly costumed people in the Piazza, as in Gentile's "Preaching of St. Mark." Not only the pleasure-loving Carpaccio, but the austere Cima, as he grew older, turned every biblical and saintly legend into an occasion for the picture of a pageant.

But there was a further reason for the popularity of such pictures. The decorations which were then being executed by the most reputed masters in the Hall of Great Council in the Doge's Palace, were, by the nature of the subject, required to represent pageants. The Venetian State encouraged painting as did the Church, in order to teach its subjects its own glory in a way that they could understand without being led on to critical enquiry. Venice was not the only city, it is true, that used painting for political purposes; but the frescoes of Lorenzetti at Siena were admonitions to govern in accordance with the Catechism, while the pictures in the Great Hall of the Doge's Palace were of a nature to remind the Venetians of their glory and also of their state policy. These mural paintings represented such subjects as the Doge bringing about a reconciliation between the Pope and the Emperor Barbarossa, an event which marked the first entry of Venice into the field of Continental politics, and typified as well its unchanging policy, which was to gain its own ends by keeping a balance of power between the allies of the Pope and the allies of his opponents. The first edition, so to speak, of these works had been executed at the end of the fourteenth century and in the beginning of the fifteenth. Toward the end of that century it no longer satisfied the new feeling for reality and beauty, and thus had ceased to serve its purpose, which was to glorify the State. The Bellini, Alvise Vivarini, and Carpaccio were employed to make a second rendering of the very same subjects, and this gave the Venetians ample opportunity for finding out how much they liked pageant pictures.

It is curious to note here that at the same time Florence also commissioned its greatest painters to execute works for its Council Hall, but left them practically free to choose their own subjects. Michelangelo chose for his theme "The Florentines while Bathing Surprised by the Pisans," and Leonardo "The Battle of the Standard." Neither of these was intended in the first place to glorify the Florentine Republic, but rather to give scope to the painter's genius, Michelangelo's for the treatment of the nude, Leonardo's for movement and animation. Each, having given scope to his peculiar talents in his cartoon, had no further interest, and neither of the undertakings was ever completed. Nor do we hear that the Florentine councillors enjoyed the cartoons, which were instantly snatched up by students who turned the hall containing them into an academy.

VI. Painting and the Confraternities.—It does not appear that the Hall of Great Council in Venice was turned into a students' academy, and, although the paintings there doubtless gave a decided incentive to artists, their effect upon the public, for whom they were designed, was even greater. The councillors were not allowed to be the only people to enjoy fascinating pictures of gorgeous pageants and ceremonials. The Mutual Aid Societies—the Schools, as they were called—were not long in getting the masters who were employed in the Doge's Palace to execute for their own meeting places pictures equally splendid. The Schools of San Giorgio, Sant' Ursula, and Santo Stefano, employed Carpaccio, the Schools of San Giovanni and San Marco, Gentile Bellini, and other Schools employed minor painters. The works carried out for these Schools are of peculiar importance, both because they are all that remain to throw light upon the pictures in the Doge's Palace destroyed in the fire of 1576, and because they form a transition to the art of a later day. Just as the State chose subjects that glorified itself and taught its own history and policy, so the Schools had pictures painted to glorify their patron saints, and to keep their deeds and example fresh. Many of these pictures—most in fact—took the form of pageants; but even in such, intended as they were for almost domestic purposes, the style of high ceremonial was relaxed, and elements taken directly from life were introduced. In his "Corpus Christi," Gentile Bellini paints not only the solemn and dazzling procession in the Piazza, but the elegant young men who strut about in all their finery, the foreign loungers, and even the unfailing beggar by the portal of St. Mark's. In his "Miracle of the True Cross," he introduces gondoliers, taking care to bring out all the beauty of their lithe, comely figures as they stand to ply the oar, and does not reject even such an episode as a serving-maid standing in a doorway watching a negro who is about to plunge into the canal. He treats this bit of the picture with all the charm and much of that delicate feeling for simple effects of light and colour that we find in such Dutch painters as Vermeer van Delft and Peter de Hoogh.

Episodes such as this in the works of the earliest great Venetian master must have acted on the public like a spark on tinder. They certainly found a sudden and assured popularity, for they play a more and more important part in the pictures executed for the Schools, many of the subjects of which were readily turned into studies of ordinary Venetian life. This was particularly true of the works of Carpaccio. Much as he loved pageants, he loved homelier scenes as well. His "Dream of St. Ursula" shows us a young girl asleep in a room filled with the quiet morning light. Indeed, it may be better described as the picture of a room with the light playing softly upon its walls, upon the flower-pots in the window, and upon the writing-table and the cupboards. A young girl happens to be asleep in the bed, but the picture is far from being a merely economic illustration to this episode in the life of the saint. Again, let us take the work in the same series where King Maure dismisses the ambassadors. Carpaccio has made this a scene of a chancellery in which the most striking features are neither the king nor the ambassadors, but the effect of the light that streams through a side door on the left and a poor clerk labouring at his task. Or, again, take St. Jerome in his study, in the Scuola di San Giorgio. He is nothing but a Venetian scholar seated in his comfortable, bright library, in the midst of his books, with his little shelf of bric-à-brac running along the wall. There is nothing in his look or surroundings to speak of a life of self-denial or of arduous devotion to the problems of sin and redemption. Even the "Presentation of the Virgin," which offered such a splendid chance for a pageant, Carpaccio, in one instance, turned into the picture of a simple girl going to her first communion. In other words, Carpaccio's quality is the quality of a painter of *genre*, of which he was the earliest Italian master. His *genre* differs from Dutch or French not in kind but in degree. Dutch *genre* is much more democratic, and, as painting, it is of a far finer quality, but it deals with its subject, as Carpaccio does, for the sake of its own pictorial capacities and for the sake of the effects of colour and of light and shade.

VII. Easel Pictures and Giorgione.—At the beginning of the Renaissance painting was almost wholly confined to the Church. From the Church it extended to the Council Hall, and thence to the Schools. There it rapidly developed into an art which had no higher aim than painting the sumptuous life of the aristocracy. When it had reached this point, there was no reason whatever why it should not begin to grace the dwellings of all well-to-do people.

In the sixteenth century painting was not looked upon with the estranging reverence paid to it now. It was almost as cheap as printing has become since, and almost as much employed. When the Venetians had attained the point of culture where they were able to differentiate their sensations and distinguish pleasure from edification, they found that painting gave them decided pleasure. Why should they always have to go to the Doge's Palace or to some School to enjoy this pleasure? That would have been no less a hardship than for us never to hear music outside of a concert-room. This is no merely rhetorical comparison, for in the life of the Venetian of the sixteenth century painting took much the same place that music takes in ours. He no longer expected it to tell him stories or to teach him the Catechism. Printed books, which were beginning to grow common, amply satisfied both these needs. He had as a rule very little personal religion, and consequently did not care for pictures that moved him to contrition or devotion. He preferred to have some pleasantly coloured thing that would put him into a mood connected with the side of life he most enjoyed—with refined merrymaking, with country parties, or with the sweet dreams of youth. Venetian painting alone among Italian schools was ready to satisfy such a demand, and it thus became the first genuinely modern art: for the most vital difference that can be indicated between the arts in antiquity and modern times is this—that now the arts tend to address themselves more and more to the actual needs of men, while in olden times they were supposed to serve some more than human purpose.

The pictures required for a house were naturally of a different kind from those suited to the Council Hall or the School, where large paintings, which could be filled with many figures, were in place. For the house smaller pictures were necessary, such as could easily be carried about. The mere dimensions, therefore, excluded pageants, but, in any case, the pageant was too formal a subject to suit all moods—too much like a brass band always playing in the room. The easel picture had to be without too definite a subject, and could no more permit being translated into words than a sonata. Some of Giovanni Bellini's late works are already of this kind. They are full of that subtle, refined poetry which can be expressed in form and colour alone. But they were a little too austere in form, a little too sober in colour, for the gay, care-free youth of the time. Carpaccio does not seem to have painted many easel pictures, although his brilliancy, his delightful fancy, his love of colour, and his gaiety of humour would have fitted him admirably for this kind of painting. But Giorgione, the follower of both these masters, starting with the qualities of both as his inheritance, combined the refined feeling and poetry of Bellini with Carpaccio's gaiety and love of beauty and colour. Stirred with the enthusiasms of his own generation as people who had lived through other phases of feeling could not be, Giorgione painted pictures so perfectly in touch with the ripened spirit of the Renaissance that they met with the success which those things only find that at the same moment wake us to the full sense of a need and satisfy it.

Giorgione's life was short, and very few of his works—not a score in all—have escaped destruction. But these suffice to give us a glimpse into that brief moment when the Renaissance found its most genuine expression in painting. Its over-boisterous passions had quieted down into a sincere appreciation of beauty and of human relations. It would be really hard to say more about Giorgione than this, that his pictures are the perfect reflex of the Renaissance at its height. His works, as well as those of his contemporaries and followers, still continue to be appreciated most by people whose attitude of mind and spirit has most in common with the Renaissance, or by those who look upon Italian art not merely as art, but as the product of this period. For that is its greatest interest. Other schools have accomplished much more in mere painting than the Italian. A serious student of art will scarcely think of putting many of even the highest achievements of the Italians, considered purely as technique, beside the works of the great Dutchmen, the great Spaniard, or even the masters of to-day. Our real interest in Italian painting is at bottom an interest in that art which we almost instinctively feel to have been the fittest expression found by a period in the history of modern Europe which has much in common with youth. The Renaissance has the fascination of those years when we seemed so full of promise both to ourselves and to everybody else.

VIII. **The Giorgionesque Spirit.**—Giorgione created a demand which other painters were forced to supply at the risk of finding no favour. The older painters accommodated themselves as best they could. One of them indeed, turning toward the new in a way that is full of singular charm, gave his later works all the beauty and softness of the first spring days in Italy. Upon hearing the title of one of Catena's works in the National Gallery, " A Warrior Adoring the Infant Christ," who could imagine what a treat the picture itself had in store for him? It is a fragrant summer landscape enjoyed by a few quiet people, one of whom, in armour, with the glamour of the Orient about him, kneels at the Virgin's feet, while a romantic young page holds his horse's bridle. I mention this picture in particular because it is so accessible, and so good an instance of the Giorgionesque way of treating a subject; not for the story, nor for the display of skill, nor for the obvious feeling, but for the lovely landscape, for the effects of light and colour, and for the sweetness of human relations. Giorgione's altar-piece at Castelfranco is treated in precisely the same spirit, but with far more genius.

The young painters had no chance at all unless they undertook at once to furnish pictures in Giorgione's style. But before we can appreciate all that the younger men were called upon to do, we must turn to the consideration of that most wonderful product of the Renaissance and of the painter's craft—the Portrait.

IX. The Portrait.—The longing for the perpetuation of one's fame, which has already been mentioned several times as one of the chief passions of the Renaissance, brought with it the more universal desire to hand down the memory of one's face and figure. The surest way to accomplish this end seemed to be the one which had proved successful in the case of the great Romans, whose effigies were growing more and more familiar as new busts and medals were dug up. The earlier generations of the Renaissance relied therefore on the sculptor and the medallist to hand down their features to an interested posterity. These artists were ready for their task. The mere materials gave them solidity, an effect so hard to get in painting. At the same time, nothing was expected from them except that they should mould the material into the desired shape. No setting was required and no colour. Their art on this account alone would naturally have been the earliest to reach fruition. But over and above this, sculptors and medallists had the direct inspiration of antique models, and through the study of these they were at an early date brought in contact with the tendencies of the Renaissance. The passion then prevailing for pronounced types, and the spirit of analysis this produced, forced them to such patient study of the face as would enable them to give the features that look of belonging to one consistent whole which we call character. Thus, at a time when painters had not yet learned to distinguish between one face and another, Donatello was carving busts which remain unrivalled as studies of character, and Pisanello was casting bronze and silver medals which are among the greatest claims to renown of those whose effigies they bear.

Donatello's bust of Niccolo d'Uzzano shows clearly, nevertheless, that the Renaissance could not long remain satisfied with the sculptured portrait. It is coloured like nature, and succeeds so well in producing for an instant the effect of actual life as to seem uncanny the next moment. Donatello's contemporaries must have had the same impression, for busts of this kind are but few. Yet these few prove that the element of colour had to be included before the satisfactory portrait was found: in other words, that painting and not sculpture was to be the portrait-art of the Renaissance.

The most creative sculptor of the earlier Renaissance was not the only artist who felt the need of colour in portraiture. Vittore Pisano, the greatest medallist of this or any age, felt it quite as keenly, and being a painter as well, he was among the first to turn this art to portraiture. In his day, however, painting was still too undeveloped an art for the portrait not to lose in character what it gained in a more lifelike colouring, and the two of Pisanello's portraits which still exist are profiles much inferior to his best medals, seeming indeed to be enlargements of them rather than original studies from life.

It was only in the next generation, when the attention of painters themselves was powerfully concentrated upon the reproduction of strongly pronounced types of humanity, that they began to make portraits as full of life and energy as Donatello's busts of the previous period. Even then, however, the full face was rarely attempted, and it was only in the beginning of the sixteenth century that full-face portraits began to be common. The earliest striking achievement of this sort, Mantegna's head of Cardinal Scarampo (now in Berlin), was not the kind to find favour in Venice. The full-face likeness of this wolf in sheep's clothing brought out the workings of the self-seeking, cynical spirit within too clearly not to have revolted the Venetians, who looked upon all such qualities as impious in the individual because they were the strict monopoly of the State. In the portraits of Doges which decorated the frieze of its great Council Hall, Venice wanted the effigies of functionaries entirely devoted to the State, and not of great personalities, and the profile lent itself more readily to the omission of purely individual traits.

It is significant that Venice was the first state which made a business of preserving the portraits of its chief rulers. Those which Gentile and Giovanni Bellini executed for this end must have had no less influence on portraiture than their mural paintings in the same Hall had on other branches of the art. But the State was not satisfied with leaving records of its glory in the Ducal Palace alone. The Church and the saints were impressed for the same purpose—happily for us, for while the portraits in the Great Hall have perished, several altar-pieces still preserve to us the likenesses of some of the Doges

Early in the sixteenth century, when people began to want pictures in their own homes as well as in their public halls, personal and religious motives combined to dictate the choice of subjects. In the minds of many, painting, although a very familiar art, was too much connected with solemn religious rites and with state ceremonies to be used at once for ends of personal pleasure. So landscape had to slide in under the patronage of St. Jerome; while romantic biblical episodes, like the "Finding of Moses," or the "Judgment of Solomon," gave an excuse for *genre*, and the portrait crept in half hidden under the mantle of a patron saint. Its position once secure, however, the portrait took no time to cast off all tutelage, and to declare itself one of the most attractive subjects possible. Over and above the obvious satisfaction afforded by a likeness, the portrait had to give pleasure to the eye, and to produce those agreeable moods which were expected from all other paintings in Giorgione's time. Portraits like that of Scarampo are scarcely less hard to live with than such a person himself must have been. They tyrannize rather than soothe and please. But Giorgione and his immediate followers painted men and women whose very look leads one to think of sympathetic friends, people whose features are pleasantly rounded, whose raiment seems soft to touch, whose surroundings call up the memory of sweet landscapes and refreshing breezes. In fact, in these portraits the least apparent object was the likeness, the real purpose being to please the eye and to turn the mind toward pleasant themes. This no doubt helps to account for the great popularity of portraits in Venice during the sixteenth century. Their number, as we shall see, only grows larger as the century advances.

X. The Young Titian.—Giorgione's followers had only to exploit the vein their master hit upon to find ample remuneration. Each, to be sure, brought a distinct personality into play, but the demand for the Giorgionesque article, if I may be allowed the phrase, was too strong to permit of much deviation. It no longer mattered what the picture was to represent or where it was going to be placed; the treatment had to be always bright, romantic, and joyous. Many artists still confined themselves to painting ecclesiastical subjects chiefly, but even among these, such painters as Lotto and Palma, for example, are fully as Giorgionesque as Titian, Bonifazio, or Paris Bordone.

Titian, in spite of a sturdier, less refined nature, did nothing for a generation after Giorgione's death but work on his lines. A difference in quality between the two masters shows itself from the first, but the spirit that animated each is identical. The pictures Titian was painting ten years after his companion's death have not only many of the qualities of Giorgione's, but something more, as if done by an older Giorgione, with better possession of himself, and with a larger and firmer hold on the world. At the same time, they show no diminution of spontaneous joy in life, and even an increased sense of its value and dignity. What an array of masterpieces might be brought to witness! In the "Assumption," for example, the Virgin soars heavenward, not helpless in the arms of angels, but borne up by the fulness of life within her, and by the feeling that the universe is naturally her own, and that nothing can check her course. The angels seem to be there only to sing the victory of a human being over his environment. They are embodied joys, acting on our nerves like the rapturous outburst of the orchestra at the end of "Parsifal." Or look at the "Bacchanals" in Madrid, or at the "Bacchus and Ariadne" in the National Gallery. How brimful they are of exuberant joy! you see no sign of a struggle of inner and outer conditions, but life so free, so strong, so glowing, that it almost intoxicates. They are truly Dionysiac, Bacchanalian triumphs—the triumph of life over the ghosts that love the gloom and chill and hate the sun.

The portraits Titian painted in these years show no less feeling of freedom from sordid cares, and no less mastery over life. Think of "The Man with the Glove" in the Louvre, of the "Concert," and "Young Englishman" in Florence, and of the Pesaro family in their altar-piece in the Frari at Venice—call up these portraits, and you will see that they are true children of the Renaissance whom life has taught no meannesses and no fears.

XI. Apparent Failure of the Renaissance.

—But even while such pictures were being painted, the spirit of the Italian Renaissance was proving inadequate to life. This was not the fault of the spirit, which was the spirit of youth. But youth cannot last more than a certain length of time. No matter how it is spent, manhood and middle age will come. Life began to show a sterner and more sober face than for a brief moment it had seemed to wear. Men became conscious that the passions for knowledge, for glory, and for personal advancement were not at the bottom of all the problems that life presented. Florence and Rome discovered this suddenly, and with a shock. In the presence of Michelangelo's sculptures in San Lorenzo, or of his "Last Judgment," we still hear the cry of anguish that went up as the inexorable truth dawned upon them. But Venice, although humiliated by the League of Cambrai, impoverished by the Turk, and by the change in the routes of commerce, was not crushed, as was the rest of Italy, under the heels of Spanish infantry, nor so drained of resource as not to have some wealth still flowing into her coffers. Life grew soberer and sterner, but it was still amply worth the living, although the relish of a little stoicism and of earnest thought no longer seemed out of place. The spirit of the Renaissance had found its way to Venice slowly; it was even more slow to depart.

We therefore find that toward the middle of the sixteenth century, when elsewhere in Italy painting was trying to adapt itself to the hypocrisy of a Church whose chief reason for surviving as an institution was that it helped Spain to subject the world to tyranny, and when portraits were already exhibiting the fascinating youths of an earlier generation turned into obsequious and elegant courtiers,—in Venice painting kept true to the ripened and more reflective spirit which succeeded to the most glowing decades of the Renaissance. This led men to take themselves more seriously, to act with more consideration of consequences, and to think of life with less hope and exultation. Quieter joys were sought, the pleasures of friendship and of the affections. Life not having proved the endless holiday it had promised to be, earnest people began to question whether under the gross masque of the official religion there was not something to console them for departed youth and for the failure of hopes. Thus religion began to revive in Italy, this time not ethnic nor political, but personal, —an answer to the real needs of the human soul.

XII. Lotto.—It is scarcely to be wondered at that the Venetian artist in whom we first find the expression of the new feelings, should have been one who by wide travel had been brought in contact with the miseries of Italy in a way not possible for those who remained sheltered in Venice. Lorenzo Lotto, when he is most himself, does not paint the triumph of man over his environment, but in his altar-pieces, and even more in his portraits, he shows us people in want of the consolations of religion, of sober thought, of friendship and affection. They look out from his canvases as if begging for sympathy.

But real expression for the new order of things was not to be found by one like Lotto, sensitive of feeling and born in the heyday of the Renaissance, to whom the new must have come as a disappointment. It had to come from one who had not been brought in personal contact with the woes of the rest of Italy, from one less conscious of his environment, one like Titian who was readier to receive the patronage of the new master than to feel an oppression which did not touch him personally; or it had to come from one like Tintoretto, born to the new order of things and not having to outlive a disappointment before adapting himself to it.

XIII. The Late Renaissance and Titian.

—It is as impossible to keep untouched by what happens to your neighbours as to have a bright sky over your own house when it is stormy everywhere else. Spain did not directly dominate Venice, but the new fashions of life and thought inaugurated by her nearly universal triumph could not be kept out. Her victims, among whom the Italian scholars must be reckoned, flocked to Venice for shelter, persecuted by a rule that cherished the Inquisition. Now for the first time Venetian painters were brought in contact with men of letters. As they were already, fortunately for themselves, too well acquainted with the business of their own art to be taken in tow by learning or even by poetry, the relation of the man of letters to the painter became on the whole a stimulating and at any rate a profitable one, as in the instance of two of the greatest, where it took the form of a partnership for mutual advantage. It is not to our purpose to speak of Aretino's gain, but Titian would scarcely have acquired such fame in his lifetime if that founder of modern journalism, Pietro Aretino, had not been at his side, eager to trumpet his praises and to advise him whom to court.

The overwhelming triumph of Spain entailed still another consequence. It brought home to all Italians, even to the Venetians, the sense of the individual's helplessness before organized power—a sense which, as we have seen, the early Renaissance, with its belief in the omnipotence of the individual, totally lacked. This was not without a decided influence on art. In the last three decades of his long career, Titian did not paint man as if he were as free from care and as fitted to his environment as a lark on an April morning. Rather did he represent man as acting on his environment and suffering from its reactions. He made the faces and figures show clearly what life had done to them. The great "Ecce Homo" and the "Crowning with Thorns" are imbued with this feeling no less than the equestrian portrait of Charles the Fifth. In the "Ecce Homo" we see a man with a godlike personality, humbled by the imperial majesty, broken by the imperial power, and utterly unable to hold out against them. In the "Crowning with Thorns" we have the same godlike being almost brutalised by pain and suffering. In the portrait of the Emperor we behold a man whom life has enfeebled, and who has to meet a foe who may crush him.

Yet Titian became neither soured nor a pessimist. Many of his late portraits are even more energetic than those of his early maturity. He shows himself a wise man of the world. "Do not be a grovelling sycophant," some of them seem to say, "but remember that courtly manners and tempered elegance can do you no harm." Titian, then, was ever ready to change with the times, and on the whole the change was toward a firmer grasp of reality, necessitating yet another advance in the painter's mastery of his craft. Titian's real greatness consists in the fact that he was as able to produce an effect of greater reality as he was ready to appreciate the need of a firmer hold on life. In painting, as I have said, a greater effect of reality is chiefly a matter of light and shadow, to be obtained only by considering the canvas as an enclosed space, filled with light and air, through which the objects are seen. There is more than one way of getting this effect, but Titian attains it by the almost total suppression of outlines, by the harmonising of his colours, and by the largeness and vigour of his brushwork. In fact, the old Titian was, in his way of painting, remarkably like some of the best French masters of to-day. This makes him only the more attractive, particularly when with handling of this kind he combined the power of creating forms of beauty such as he has given us in the " Wisdom " of the Venetian Royal Palace, or in the "Shepherd and Nymph" of Vienna. The difference between the old Titian, author of these works, and the young Titian, painter of the "Assumption," and of the "Bacchus and Ariadne," is the difference between the Shakspeare of the "Midsummer-Night's Dream" and the Shakspeare of the "Tempest." Titian and Shakspeare begin and end so much in the same way by no mere accident. They were both products of the Renaissance, they underwent similar changes, and each was the highest and completest expression of his own age. This is not the place to elaborate the comparison, but I have dwelt so long on Titian, because, historically considered, he is the only painter who expressed nearly all of the Renaissance that could find expression in painting. It is this which makes him even more interesting than Tintoretto, an artist who in many ways was deeper, finer, and even more brilliant.

XIV. Humanity and the Renaissance.— Tintoretto grew to manhood when the fruit of the Renaissance was ripe on every bough.

The Renaissance had resulted in the emancipation of the individual, in making him feel that the universe had no other purpose than his happiness. This brought an entirely new answer to the question, "Why should I do this or that?" It used to be, "Because self-instituted authority commands you." The answer now was, "Because it is good for men." In this lies our greatest debt to the Renaissance, that it instituted the welfare of man as the end of all action. The Renaissance did not bring this idea to practical issue, but our debt to it is endless on account of the results the idea has produced in our own days. This alone would have made the Renaissance a period of peculiar interest, even if it had had no art whatever. But when ideas are fresh and strong, they are almost sure to find artistic embodiment, as indeed this whole epoch found in painting, and this particular period in the works of Tintoretto.

XV. Sebastiano del Piombo.—The emancipation of the individual had a direct effect on the painter in freeing him from his guild.

It now occurred to him that possibly he might become more proficient and have greater success if he deserted the influences he was under by the accident of birth and residence, and placed himself in the school that seemed best adapted to foster his talents. This led to the unfortunate experiment of Eclecticism which checked the purely organic development of the separate schools. It brought about their fusion into an art which no longer appealed to the Italian people, as did the art which sprang naturally from the soil, but to the small class of *dilettanti* who considered a knowledge of art as one of the birthrights of their social position. Venice, however, suffered little from Eclecticism, perhaps because a strong sense of individuality was late in getting there, and by that time the painters were already well enough educated in their craft to know that they had little to learn elsewhere. The one Venetian who became an Eclectic, remained in spite of it a great painter. Sebastiano del Piombo fell under the influence of Michelangelo, but while this influence was pernicious in most cases, the hand that had learned to paint under Bellini, Cima, and Giorgione, never wholly lost its command of colour and tone.

XVI. Tintoretto.—Tintoretto stayed at home, but he felt in his own person a craving for something that Titian could not teach him. The Venice he was born in was not the Venice of Titian's early youth, and his own adolescence fell in the period when Spain was rapidly making herself mistress of Italy. The haunting sense of powers almost irresistible gave a terrible fascination to Michelangelo's works, which are swayed by that sense as by a demonic presence. Tintoretto felt this fascination because he was in sympathy with the spirit which took form in colossal torsoes and limbs. To him these were not, as they were to Michelangelo's enrolled followers, merely new patterns after which to model the nude.

But beside this sense of overwhelming power and gigantic force, Tintoretto had to an even greater degree the feeling that whatever existed was for mankind and with reference to man. In his youth people were once more turning to religion, and in Venice poetry was making its way more than it had previously done, not only because Venice had become the refuge of men of letters, but also because of the diffusion of printed books. Tintoretto took to the new feeling for religion and poetry as to his birthright. Yet whether classic fable or biblical episode were the subject of his art, Tintoretto coloured it with his feeling for the human life at the heart of the story. His sense of power did not express itself in colossal nudes so much as in the immense energy, in the glowing health of the figures he painted, and more still in his effects of light, which he rendered as if he had it in his hands to brighten or darken the heavens at will and subdue them to his own moods.

He could not have accomplished this, we may be sure, if he had not had even greater skill than Titian in the treatment of light and shadow and of atmosphere. It was this which enabled him to give such living versions of biblical stories and saintly legends. For, granting that an effect of reality were attainable in painting without an adequate treatment of light and atmosphere, even then, the reality would look hideous, as it does in many modern painters who attempt to paint people of to-day in their every-day dress and among their usual surroundings. It is not "Realism" which makes such pictures hideous, but the want of that toning down which the atmosphere gives to things in life, and of that harmonising to which the light subjects all colours.

It was a great mastery of light and shadow which enabled Tintoretto to put into his pictures all the poetry there was in his soul without once tempting us to think that he might have found better expression in words. The poetry which quickens most of his works in the Scuola di San Rocco is almost entirely a matter of light and colour. What is it but the light that changes the solitudes in which the Magdalen and St. Mary of Egypt are sitting, into dreamlands seen by poets in their moments of happiest inspiration? What but light and colour, the gloom and chill of evening, with the white-stoled figure standing resignedly before the judge, that give the "Christ before Pilate" its sublime magic? What, again, but light, colour, and the star-procession of cherubs that imbue the realism of the "Annunciation" with music which thrills us through and through?

Religion and poetry did not exist for Tintoretto because the love and cultivation of the Muses was a duty prescribed by the Greeks and Romans, and because the love of God and the saints was prescribed by the Church; but rather, as was the case with the best people of his time, because both poetry and religion were useful to man. They helped him to forget what was mean and sordid in life, they braced him to his task, and consoled him for his disappointments. Religion answered to an ever-living need of the human heart. The Bible was no longer a mere document wherewith to justify Christian dogma. It was rather a series of parables and symbols pointing at all times to the path that led to a finer and nobler life. Why then continue to picture Christ and the Apostles, the Patriarchs and Prophets, as persons living under Roman rule, wearing the Roman toga, and walking about in the landscape of a Roman bas-relief? Christ and the

Apostles, the Patriarchs and Prophets, were the embodiment of living principles and of living ideals. Tintoretto felt this so vividly that he could not think of them otherwise than as people of his own kind, living under conditions easily intelligible to himself and to his fellow-men. Indeed, the more intelligible and the more familiar the look and garb and surroundings of biblical and saintly personages, the more would they drive home the principles and ideas they incarnated. So Tintoretto did not hesitate to turn every biblical episode into a picture of what the scene would look like had it taken place under his own eyes, nor to tinge it with his own mood.

His conception of the human form was, it is true, colossal, although the slender elegance that was then coming into fashion, as if in protest against physical force and organisation, influenced him considerably in his construction of the female figure; but the effect which he must always have produced upon his contemporaries, and which most of his works still produce, is one of astounding reality as well as of wide sweep and power. Thus, in the "Discovery of the Body of St. Mark," in the Brera, and in the "Storm Rising while the Corpse is being Carried through the Streets of Alexandria," in the Royal Palace at Venice, the figures, although colossal, are so energetic and so easy in movement, and the effects of perspective and of light and atmosphere are so on a level with the gigantic figures, that the eye at once adapts itself to the scale, and you feel as if you too partook of the strength and health of heroes.

XVII. Value of Minor Episodes in Art.— That feeling for reality which made the great painters look upon a picture as the representation of a cubic content of atmosphere enveloping all the objects depicted, made them also consider the fact that the given quantity of atmosphere is sure to contain other objects than those the artist wants for his purpose. He is free to leave them out, of course, but in so far as he does, so far is he from producing an effect of reality. The eye does not see everything, but all the eye would naturally see along with the principal objects, must be painted, or the picture will not look true to life. This incorporation of small episodes running parallel with the subject rather than forming part of it, is one of the chief characteristics of modern as distinguished from ancient art. It is this which makes the Elizabethan drama so different from the Greek. It is this again which already separates the works of Duccio and Giotto from the plastic arts of Antiquity. Painting lends itself willingly to the consideration of minor episodes, and for that reason is almost as well fitted to be in touch with modern life as the novel itself. Such a treatment saves a picture from looking prepared and cold, just as light and atmosphere save it from rigidity and crudeness.

No better illustration of this can be found among Italian masters than Tintoretto's "Crucifixion" in the Scuola di San Rocco. The scene is a vast one, and although Christ is on the Cross, life does not stop. To most of the people gathered there, what takes place is no more than a common execution. Many of them are attending to it as to a tedious duty. Others work away at some menial task more or less connected with the Crucifixion, as unconcerned as cobblers humming over their last. Most of the people in the huge canvas are represented, as no doubt they were in life, without much personal feeling about Christ. His own friends are painted with all their grief and despair, but the others are allowed to feel as they please. The painter does not try to give them the proper emotions. If one of the great novelists of to-day, if Tolstoi, for instance, were to describe the Crucifixion, his account would read as if it were a description of Tintoretto's picture. But Tintoretto's fairness went even further than letting all the spectators feel as they pleased about what he himself believed to be the greatest event that ever took place. Among this multitude he allowed the light of heaven to shine upon the wicked as well as upon the good, and the air to refresh them all equally. In other words, this enormous canvas is a great sea of air and light at the bottom of which the scene takes place. Without the atmosphere and the just distribution of light, it would look as lifeless and desolate, in spite of the crowd and animation, as if it were the bottom of a dried up sea.

XVIII. Tintoretto's Portraits.—While all these advances were being made, the art of portraiture had not stood still. Its popularity had only increased as the years went on. Titian was too busy with commissions for foreign princes to supply the great demand there was in Venice alone. Tintoretto painted portraits not only with much of the air of good breeding of Titian's likenesses, but with even greater splendour, and with an astonishing rapidity of execution. The Venetian portrait, it will be remembered, was expected to be more than a likeness. It was expected to give pleasure to the eye, and to stimulate the emotions. Tintoretto was ready to give ample satisfaction to all such expectations. His portraits, although they are not so individualised as Lotto's, nor such close studies of character as Titian's, always render the man at his best, in glowing health, full of life and determination. They give us the sensuous pleasure we get from jewels, and at the same time they make us look back with amazement to a State where the human plant was in such vigour as to produce old men of the kind represented in most of Tintoretto's portraits.

With Tintoretto ends the universal interest the Venetian school arouses; for although painting does not deteriorate in a day any more than it grows to maturity in the same brief moment, the story of the decay has none of the fascination of the growth. But several artists remain to be considered who were not of the Venetian school in the strict sense of the term, but who have always been included within it.

XIX. Venetian Art and the Provinces.— The Venetian provinces were held together not merely by force of rule. In language and feeling no less than in government, they formed a distinct unit within the Italian peninsula. Painting being so truly a product of the soil as it was in Italy during the Renaissance, the art of the provinces could not help holding the same close relation to the art of Venice that their language and modes of feeling held. But a difference must be made at once between towns like Verona, with a school of at least as long a growth and with as independent an evolution as the school of Venice itself, and towns like Vicenza and Brescia whose chief painters never developed quite independently of Venice or Verona. What makes Romanino and Moretto of Brescia, or even the powerful Montagna of Vicenza, except when they are at their very best, so much less enjoyable as a rule than the Venetians—that is to say the painters wholly educated in Venice,—is something they have in common with the Eclectics of a later day. They are ill at ease about their art, which is no longer the utterly unpremeditated outcome of a natural impulse. They saw greater painting than their own in Venice and Verona, and not unfrequently their own works show an uncouth attempt to adopt that greatness, which comes out in exaggeration of colour even more than of form, and speaks for that want of taste which is the indelible stamp of provincialism. But there were Venetian towns without the traditions even of the schools of Vicenza and Brescia, where, if you wanted to learn painting, you had to apprentice yourself to somebody who had been taught by somebody who had been a pupil of one of Giovanni Bellini's pupils. This was particularly true of the towns in that long stretch of plain between the Julian Alps and the sea, known as Friuli. Friuli produced one painter of remarkable talents and great force, Giovanni Antonio Pordenone, but neither his talents nor his force, nor even later study in Venice, could erase from his works that stamp of provincialism which he inherited from his first provincial master.

Such artists as these, however, never gained great favour in the capital. Those whom Venice drew to herself when her own strength was waning and when, like Rome in her decline, she began to absorb into herself the talent of the provinces, were rather painters such as Paolo Veronese whose art, although of independent growth, was sufficiently like her own to be readily understood, or painters with an entirely new vein, such as the Bassani.

XX. **Paul Veronese.**—Paolo was the product of four or five generations of Veronese painters, the first two or three of which had spoken the language of the whole mass of the people in a way that few other artists had ever done. Consequently, in the early Renaissance, there were no painters in the North of Italy, and few even in Florence, who were not touched by the influence of the Veronese. But Paolo's own immediate predecessors were no longer able to speak the language of the whole mass of the people. There was one class they left out entirely, the class to whom Titian and Tintoretto appealed so strongly, the class that ruled, and that thought in the new way. Verona, being a dependency of Venice, did no ruling, and certainly not at all so much thinking as Venice, and life there continued healthful, simple, unconscious, untroubled by the approaching storm in the world's feelings. But although thought and feeling may be slow in invading a town, fashion comes there quickly. Spanish fashions in dress, and Spanish ceremonial in manners reached Verona soon enough, and in Paolo Caliari we find all these fashions reflected, but health, simplicity, and unconsciousness as well. This combination of seemingly opposite qualities forms his great charm for us to-day, and it must have proved as great an attraction to many of the Venetians of his own time, for they were already far enough removed from simplicity to appreciate to the full his singularly happy combination of ceremony and splendour with an almost childlike naturalness of feeling. Perhaps among his strongest admirers were the very men who most appreciated Titian's distinction and Tintoretto's poetry. But it is curious to note that Paolo's chief employers were the monasteries. His cheerfulness, and his frank and joyous worldliness, the qualities, in short, which we find in his huge pictures of feasts, seem to have been particularly welcome to those who were expected to make their meat and drink of the very opposite qualities. This is no small comment on the times, and shows how thorough had been the permeation of the spirit of the Renaissance when even the religious orders gave up their pretence to asceticism and piety.

XXI. Bassano, Genre, and Landscape.—
Venetian painting would not have been the

complete expression of the riper Renaissance if it had entirely neglected the country. City people have a natural love of the country, but when it was a matter of doubt whether a man would ever return if he ventured out of the town-gates, as was the case in the Middle Ages, this love had no chance of showing itself. It had to wait until the country itself was safe for wayfarers, a state of things which came about in Italy with the gradual submission of the country to the rule of the neighbouring cities and with the general advance of civilisation. During the Renaissance the love of the country and its pleasures received an immense impulse from Latin authors. What the great Romans without exception recommended, an Italian was not slow to adopt, particularly when, as in this case, it harmonised with natural inclination and with an already common practice. It was the usual thing with those who could afford to do so to retire to the villa for a large part of the year. Classic poets helped such Italians to appreciate the simplicity of the country and to feel a little of its beauty. Many took such delight in country life that they wished to have reminders of it in town. It may have been in response to some such half formulated wish that Palma began to paint his "Sante Conversazioni,"—groups of saintly personages gathered under pleasant trees in pretty landscapes. His pupil, Bonifazio, continued the same line, gradually, however, discarding the traditional group of Madonna and saints, and, under such titles as "The Rich Man's Feast" or "The Finding of Moses," painting all the scenes of fashionable country life, music on the terrace of a villa, hunting parties, and picnics in the forest.

Bonifazio's pupil, Jacopo Bassano, no less fond of painting country scenes, did not however confine himself to representing city people in their parks. His pictures were for the inhabitants of the small market-town from which he takes his name, where inside the gates you still see men and women in rustic garb crouching over their many-coloured wares; and where, just outside the walls, you may see all the ordinary occupations connected with farming and grazing. Inspired, although unawares, by the new idea of giving perfectly modern versions of biblical stories, Bassano introduced into nearly every picture he painted episodes from the life in the streets of Bassano, and in the county just outside the gates. Even Orpheus in his hands becomes a farmer's lad fiddling to the barnyard fowls.

Bassano's pictures and those of his two sons, who followed him very closely, found great favour in Venice and elsewhere, because they were such unconscious renderings of simple country life, a kind of life whose charm seemed greater and greater the more fashionable and ceremonious private life in the city became. But this was far from being their only charm. Just as the Church had educated people to understand painting as a language, so the love of all the pleasant things that painting suggested led in time to the love of this art as its own end, serving no obvious purpose either of decoration or suggestion, but giving pleasure by the skilful management of light and shadow, and by the intrinsic beauty of the colours. The third quarter of the sixteenth century thus saw the rise of the picture-fancier, and the success of the Bassani was so great because they appealed to this class in a special way. In Venice there had long been a love of objects for their sensuous beauty. At an early date the Venetians had perfected an art in which there is scarcely any intellectual content whatever, and in which colour, jewel-like or opaline, is almost everything. Venetian glass was at the same time an outcome of the Venetians' love of sensuous beauty and a continual stimulant to it. Pope Paul II., for example, who was a Venetian, took such a delight in the colour and glow of jewels, that he was always looking at them and always handling them. When painting, accordingly, had reached the point where it was no longer dependent upon the Church, nor even expected to be decorative, but when it was used purely for pleasure, the day could not be far distant when people would expect painting to give them the same enjoyment they received from jewels and glass. In Bassano's works this taste found full satisfaction. Most of his pictures seem at first as dazzling, then as cooling and soothing, as the best kind of stained glass; while the colouring of details, particularly of those under high lights, is jewel-like, as clear and deep and satisfying as rubies and emeralds.

It need scarcely be added after all that has been said about light and atmosphere in connection with Titian and Tintoretto, and their handling of real life, that Bassano's treatment of both was even more masterly. If this were not so, neither picture-fanciers of his own time, nor we nowadays, should care for his works as we do. They represent life in far more humble phases than even the pictures of Tintoretto, and, without recompensing effects of light and atmosphere, they would not be more enjoyable than the cheap work of the smaller Dutch masters. It must be added, too, that without his jewel-like colouring, Bassano would often be no more delightful than Teniers.

Another thing Bassano could not fail to do, working as he did in the country, and for country people, was to paint landscape. He had to paint the real country, and his skill in the treatment of light and atmosphere was great enough to enable him to do it well. Bassano was in fact the first modern landscape painter. Titian and Tintoretto and Giorgione, and even Bellini and Cima before them, had painted beautiful landscapes, but they were seldom direct studies from nature. They were decorative backgrounds, or fine harmonising accompaniments to the religious or human elements of the picture. They never failed to get grand and effective lines—a setting worthy of the subject. Bassano did not need such setting for his country versions of Bible stories, and he needed them even less in his studies of rural life. For pictures of this kind the country itself naturally seemed the best background and the best accompaniment possible,—indeed, the only kind desirable. Without knowing it, therefore, and without intending it, Bassano was the first Italian who tried to paint the country as it really is, and not arranged to look like scenery.

XXII. The Venetians and Velasquez.—Had Bassano's qualities, however, been of the kind that appealed only to the collectors of his time, he would scarcely rouse the strong interest we take in him. We care for him chiefly because he has so many of the more essential qualities of great art—truth to life, and spontaneity. He has another interest still, in that he began to beat out the path which ended at last in Velasquez. Indeed, one of the attractions of the Venetian school of painting is that, more than all others, it went to form that great Spanish master. He began as a sort of follower of Bassano, but his style was not fixed before he had given years of study to Veronese, to Tintoretto, and to Titian.

XXIII. Decline of Venetian Art.—Bassano appealed to collectors by mere accident. He certainly did not work for them. The painters who came after him and after Tintoretto no longer worked unconsciously, as Veronese did, nor for the whole intelligent class, as Titian and Tintoretto had done, but for people who prided themselves on their connoisseurship.

Palma the Younger and Domenico Tintoretto began well enough as natural followers of Tintoretto, but before long they became aware of their inferiority to the masters who had preceded them, and, feeling no longer the strength to go beyond them, fell back upon painting variations of those pictures of Tintoretto and Titian which had proved most popular. So their works recall the great masters, but only to bring out their own weakness. Padovanino, Liberi, and Pietro della Vecchia went even lower down and shamelessly manufactured pictures which, in the distant markets for which they were intended, passed for works of Titian, Veronese, and Giorgione. Nor are these pictures altogether unenjoyable. There are airs by the great composers we so love that we enjoy them even when woven into the compositions of some third-rate master.

XXIV. Longhi.—But Venetian painting was not destined to die unnoticed. In the eighteenth century, before the Republic entirely disappeared, Venice produced three or four painters who deserve at the least a place with the best painters of that century. The constitution of the Venetian State had remained unchanged. Magnificent ceremonies still took place, Venice was still the most splendid and the most luxurious city in the world. If the splendour and luxury were hollow, they were not more so than elsewhere in Europe. The eighteenth century had the strength which comes from great self-confidence and profound satisfaction with one's surroundings. It was so self-satisfied that it could not dream of striving to be much better than it was. Everything was just right; there seemed to be no great issues, no problems arising that human intelligence untrammelled by superstition could not instantly solve. Everybody was therefore in holiday mood, and the gaiety and frivolity of the century were of almost as much account as its politics and culture. There was no room for great distinctions. Hair-dressers and tailors found as much consideration as philosophers and statesmen at a lady's levee. People were delighted with their own occupations, their whole lives; and whatever people delight in, that they will have represented in art. The love for pictures was by no means dead in Venice, and Longhi painted for the picture-loving Venetians their own lives in all their ordinary domestic and fashionable phases. In the hair-dressing scenes we hear the gossip of the periwigged barber; in the dressmaking scenes, the chatter of the maid; in the dancing-school, the pleasant music of the violin. There is no tragic note anywhere. Everybody dresses, dances, makes bows, takes coffee, as if there were nothing else in the world that wanted doing. A tone of high courtesy, of great refinement, coupled with an all-pervading cheerfulness, distinguishes Longhi's pictures from the works of Hogarth, at once so brutal and so full of presage of change.

XXV. Canaletto and Guardi.—Venice herself had not grown less beautiful in her decline. Indeed, the building which occupies the very centre of the picture Venice leaves in the mind, the Salute, was not built until the seventeenth century. This was the picture that the Venetian himself loved to have painted for him, and that the stranger wanted to carry away. Canale painted Venice with a feeling for space and atmosphere, with a mastery over the delicate effects of mist peculiar to the city, that make his views of the

Salute, the Grand Canal, and the Piazzetta still seem more like Venice than all the pictures of them that have been painted since. Later in the century Canale was followed by Guardi, who executed smaller views with more of an eye for the picturesque, and for what may be called instantaneous effects, thus anticipating both the Romantic and the Impressionist painters of our own century.

XXVI. Tiepolo.—But delightful as Longhi, Canale, and Guardi are, and imbued as they are with the spirit of their own century, they lack the quality of force, without which there can be no really impressive style. This quality their contemporary Tiepolo possessed to the utmost. His energy, his feeling for splendour, his mastery over his craft, place him almost on a level with the great Venetians of the sixteenth century, although he never allows one to forget what he owes to them, particularly to Veronese. The grand scenes he paints differ from those of his predecessor not so much in mere inferiority of workmanship, as in a lack of that simplicity and candour which never failed Paolo, no matter how proud the event he might be portraying. Tiepolo's people are haughty, as if they felt that to keep a firm hold on their dignity they could not for a moment relax their faces and figures from a monumental look and bearing. They evidently feel themselves so superior that they are not pleasant to live with, although they carry themselves so well, and are dressed with such splendour, that once in a while it is a great pleasure to look at them. It was Tiepolo's vision of the world that was at fault, and his vision of the world was at fault only because the world itself was at fault. Paolo saw a world touched only by the fashions of the Spanish Court, while Tiepolo lived among people whose very hearts had been vitiated by its measureless haughtiness.

But Tiepolo's feeling for strength, for movement, and for colour was great enough to give a new impulse to art. At times he seems not so much the last of the old masters as the first of the new. The works he left in Spain do more than a little to explain the revival of painting in that country under Goya;

and Goya, in his turn, had a great influence upon many of the best French artists of our own times.

XXVII. Influence of Venetian Art.— Thus, Venetian painting before it wholly died, flickered up again strong enough to light the torch that is burning so steadily now. Indeed, not the least attraction of the Venetian masters is their note of modernity, by which I mean the feeling they give us that they were on the high road to the art of to-day. We have seen how on two separate occasions Venetian painters gave an impulse to Spaniards, who in turn have had an extraordinary influence on modern painting. It would be easy, too, although it is not my purpose, to show how much other schools of the seventeenth and eighteenth centuries, such as the Flemish, led by Rubens, and the English led by Reynolds, owed to the Venetians. My endeavour has been to explain some of the attractions of the school, and particularly to show its close dependence upon the thought and feeling of the Renaissance. This is perhaps its greatest interest, for being such a complete expression of the riper spirit of the Renaissance, it helps us to a larger understanding of a period which has in itself the fascination of youth, and which is particularly attractive to us, because the spirit that animates us is singularly like the better spirit of that epoch. We, too, are possessed of boundless curiosity. We, too, have an almost intoxicating sense of human capacity. We, too, believe in a great future for humanity, and nothing has yet happened to check our delight in discovery or our faith in life.

INDEX TO THE WORKS OF THE PRINCIPAL VENETIAN PAINTERS.

NOTE.

Public galleries are mentioned first, then private collections, and churches last. The principal public gallery is always understood after the simple mention of a city or town. Thus, Paris means Paris, Louvre, London means London, National Gallery, etc.

An interrogation point after the number or title of a picture indicates that its attribution to the given painter is doubtful.

Distinctly early or late works are marked E. or L.

It need scarcely be said that the attributions here given are not based on official catalogues, and are often at variance with them.

ANTONELLO DA MESSINA.

B. Circa 1444 : d. circa 1493. Began under unknown Flemish painter; influenced by the Vivarini and Bellini.

Antwerp.   4. Crucifixion, 1475.
Bergamo.   LOCHIS, 222. St. Sebastian.
Berlin.   18. Portrait of Young Man, 1478.
           18ᴬ. Portrait of Young Man, 1474.
           25. Portrait of Young Man in Red Coat.
Dresden.   52. St. Sebastian.

London.	673. The Saviour, 1465. 1141. Portrait of Man. 1166. Crucifixion, 1477. 1418. St. Jerome in his Study.
Messina.	Madonna with SS. Gregory and Benedict, 1473.
Milan.	MUSEO CIVICO, 95. Portrait of Man wearing Wreath.
	PRINCE TRIVULZIO, Portrait of Man, 1476.
Naples.	SALA GRANDE, 16. Portrait of Man.
Paris.	1134. Condottiere, 1474.
Rome.	VILLA BORGHESE, 396. Portrait of Man.
Venice.	ACADEMY, 589. Ecce Homo.
	GIOVANELLI, Portrait of Man.
Vicenza.	SALA IV, 17. Christ at Column.

JACOPO DI BARBARI.

1450 circa–1516 circa. Pupil of Alvise Vivarini; influenced by Antonello da Messina.

Augsburg.	Still Life Piece, 1504.
Bergamo.	GALLERY LOCHIS, 147, 148. Heads of Young Men.
	FRIZZONI-SALIS, Head of Christ.
Berlin.	26ᴬ. Madonna and Saints.
Dresden.	57. Christ Blessing.
	58, 59. SS. Catherine and Barbara.
	294. Galatea. L.
Florence.	PITTI, 384. St. Sebastian.
Hamburg.	CONSUL WEBER, 24. Old Man and Young Woman. 1503.
London.	MR. DOETSCH, Portrait of Young Man. L.
Naples.	SALA DEGLI OLANDESI E TEDESCHI, 51. Bust of a Cardinal.
Treviso.	S. NICCOLÒ, Frescoes around Tomb of Onigo.
	18 PIAZZA DEL DUOMO, Frescoes on Façade.

THE VENETIAN PAINTERS. 81

Venice.   LADY LAYARD, A Falcon.
          FRARI, 2d CHAPEL L. OF CHOIR, Decorative
            Frescoes.
Vienna.   22. Portrait of Young Man.
Weimar.   Head of Christ.

BARTOLOMMEO VENETO.

Active 1505-1555. Pupil of Gentile Bellini; influenced by Bergamask and Milanese painters.

Belluno.   22. Madonna.
Bergamo.   CARRARA, 185. Landscape. E.
            LOCHIS, 127. Madonna, 1505.
Brussels.   M. LÉON SOMZÉE, Bust of a Venetian Noble.
Douai.   324. Portrait of Young Man.
Dresden.   292. Salome.
Florence.   UFFIZI, 650. Portrait of a Man, 1555.
Frankfort. 13. Portrait of a Courtesan.
            20. St. Catherine.
Genoa.   PRINCE GIORGIO DORIA, Portrait of a Lady.
Glasgow.   510. St. Catherine crowned.
London.   287. Portrait of Ludovico Martinengo, 1530.
            MR. BENSON, Madonna and Angels. E.
            DORCHESTER HOUSE, Portrait of Man, 1512.
Milan.   AMBROSIANA, 24. Madonna. Portrait of Man
              in Black.
            BORROMEO, St. Catherine.
            DUKE MELZI, Jewess breaking her Wedding
              Ring.
Nancy.   Portrait of Young Man.
Paris.   1673. Portrait of Lady.
Rome.   CORSINI, 610. Portrait of Young Man.
            DORIA, 482. The Saviour.
Venice.   PALAZZO DUCALE, CHAPEL, Madonna.
Verona.   Madonna. E.

WORKS OF

MARCO BASAITI.

Circa 1470–1527. Pupil of Alvise Vivarini ; follower of Bellini.
Badger Hall (Shropshire). MR. F. CAPEL-CURE, Bust of Boy.
Bergamo. CARRARA, 165. The Saviour, 1517.
    LOCHIS, 188. Portrait of Man.
    MORELLI, Portrait of Man, 1521.
    FRIZZONI-SALIS, Madonna with SS. Monica and Francis.
Berlin. 6. Pietà. E. 20. Altar-piece. 37. St. Sebastian. 40. Madonna. E.
    HERR VON BECKERATH, St. Jerome.
    HERR KAUFMANN, St. Jerome.
Boston, U. S. A. 35. Entombment. E.
Buda-Pesth. 103. St. Catherine Reading. St. Jerome.
London. 281. St. Jerome. 599. Madonna.
    MR. BENSON, St. Jerome beside a Pool, 1505. Portrait of Man. Madonna and Saints. Infant Bacchus.
    MR. C. BUTLER, Dead Christ.
    MR. SALTING, Madonna. E.
    SIR MICHAEL SHAW-STEWART, Madonna.
Meiningen. DUCAL PALACE, St. Antony Abbot. St. Paul. L.
Milan. AMBROSIANA, 30. Resurrected Christ.
Munich. 1031. Madonna, Saints, and Donor. E.
Murano. S. PIETRO, Assumption of Virgin.
Padua. SALA EMO, 225. Portrait of Man 1521. Madonna with SS. Liberale and Peter.
Paris. M. MARTIN LE ROY, St. Sebastian.
Rome. DORIA, 459. St. Sebastian.
Strassburg. St. Jerome.
Stuttgart. 24. Madonna.
    57. Madonna with female Saint.

THE VENETIAN PAINTERS. 83

Venice. ACADEMY, 68. St. James and St. Antony Abbot. 108. Dead Christ. St. George and Dragon, 1520. 69. Christ in the Garden 1510. 107. St. Jerome. 39. Calling of Children of Zebedee, 1510.
MUSEO CORRER, SALA IX, 24. Madonna and Donor. 34. Christ and Angels.
GIOVANELLI, St. Jerome in Desert.
S. PIETRO IN CASTELLO, St. Peter enthroned and four other Saints.
SALUTE, St. Sebastian.

Vienna. 1. Calling of Children of Zebedee, 1515.
HARRACH COLLECTION, Madonna.

JACOPO BASSANO.

1510-1592. Pupil of Bonifazio Veronese.

Ashridge. LORD BROWNLOW, Portrait of an Admiral. Portrait of Youth.
Augsburg. 272. Madonna with SS. John and Roch.
Bassano. 32. Susanna and Elders. E.
35. Christ and Adulteress. E.
38. The Three Holy Children. E.
41. Madonna, SS. Lucy and Francis, and Donor. E.
22. Flight into Egypt. E.
20. St. John the Baptist.
19. Paradise.
17. Baptism of St. Lucilla.
16. Adoration of Shepherds.
14. St. Martin and the Beggar.
12. St. Roch recommending Donor to Virgin.
13. St. John the Evangelist adored by a Warrior.
10. Descent of Holy Spirit.
4. Madonna in Glory, SS. Lucy and Agatha. L.
45. Last Supper.

Bassano (*Con.*). DUOMO, St. Lucy in Glory, and Martyrdom of Stephen. L. Nativity.
S. GIOVANNI, Madonna in Glory, SS. Giustina, Barbara, and Mark.
S. M. DELLE GRAZIE, Crucifixion (fresco).
Bergamo. CARRARA, 109. Male Portrait.
LOCHIS, 54. Portrait of Lawyer. 82. Portrait of a Painter.
FRIZZONI-SALIS, Madonna. Portrait of Old Man.
SIGNOR BAGLIONI, Portrait of Old Man.
CASA SUARDI, St. Jerome in Desert.
Berlin. HERR KAUFMANN, Bust of Senator.
HERR WESENDONCK, Animals going into Ark.
Biel, N. B. MRS. HAMILTON OGILVIE, Dives and Lazarus. Nativity. L.
Bologna. CORRIDOR IV, Two Male Busts.
Brussels. 401. Old Man seated.
Buda-Pesth. 108. Head of St. Jerome.
Chatsworth. DUKE OF DEVONSHIRE, Portrait of Niccolo Cappello.
Cittadella. DUOMO, Christ at Emaus. E.
Dijon. 40. Agony in Garden.
41. St. Sebastian.
Dresden. 253. Israelites in Desert. 256. Moses striking Rock.
258. Conversion of Paul.
Edinburgh. 327. Portrait of Man.
367. Adoration of Magi. E.
Feltre. VESCOVADO, Portrait of Old Man.
Florence. UFFIZI, 610. Two Hunting Dogs.
Gosford House, N. B. LORD WEMYS, Bust of Old Man. Senator seated. St. John in Landscape.
Hampton Court. 94. Head of Old Man.
136. Male Portrait.
142. Jacob's Journey.

THE VENETIAN PAINTERS. 85

Hampton Court (*Con.*). 153. Boaz and Ruth.
    163. Shepherds' Offering. E.
    169. Christ in the House of the Pharisee.
    176. Assumption of Virgin.
    210. Men fighting Bears.
    223. Tribute Money.
Hopetoun House, N. B. LORD HOPETOUN, Portrait of a Doge Seated.
Linlathen, N. B. COL. ERSKINE, Agony in Garden.
London.   173. Portrait of Man. 228. Christ and the Money Changers. 277. The Good Samaritan.
    MR. BENSON, St. John in the Wilderness. Christ in House of Levi. Portrait of Woman.
    MR. G. DONALDSON, Portrait of Man aged 27, 1558.
Milan.   AMBROSIANA, 226. Annunciation to Shepherds. L. 230. Adoration of Shepherds. E.
Modena.   422. St. Paul and another Saint.
Montpellier. 564. Old Man in Armour.
Munich.   1128. Old Man, Son, and Grandson. 1148. St. Jerome in Desert. 1150. Deposition from Cross. 1151. Madonna enthroned and two Saints.
    LOTZBECK COLLECTION, 101. Portrait of Lady.
Padua.   S. MARIA IN VANZO, Entombment.
Paris.   1428. Vintage. L. 1429. Portrait of Giovanni da Bologna. 1467. Portrait of Old Man.
Rome.   VILLA BORGHESE, 144. Last Supper. 127. The Trinity.
    CORSINI, 533. Portrait of Lady.
    COUNTESS SANTA FIORA, Nativity.
Rossie Priory, N. B. LORD KINNAIRD, Annunciation.
Tours.   4. Bust of Old Man.

WORKS OF

Venice. ACADEMY, 395. Christ in Garden. 403. Portrait of a Venetian Noble. 401. St. Eleuterius blessing the Faithful.
PALAZZO DUCALE, ANTI-COLLEGIO. Jacob's Journey.
PALAZZO REALE, St. Jerome, 1569.
S. GIACOMO DALL' ORIO, Madonna in Glory and two Saints.

Verona. 214. Portrait of a Senator.

Vicenza. SALA V, Madonna and Saints. E.
ENTRANCE HALL, 2. Madonna, St. Mark, and two Senators.
PALAZZO LOSCHI, Night Scene.

Vienna. 283. The Good Samaritan.
269. Thamar led to the Stake.
276. Adoration of Magi.
301. Rich Man and Lazarus.
266. The Lord shows Abraham the Promised Land.
306. The Sower.
281. A Hunt.
319. Way to Golgotha.
268. Noah entering the Ark.
267. Christ and the Money Changers.
265. After the Flood.
263. SS. Sebastian, Florian, and Roch.
272. Adoration of Magi.
311. Portrait of Procurator.
312. Portrait of Senator.
453. Christ bearing Cross.
230. Two Men.
240. Portrait of Young Man.
480. Portrait of Young Man.
ACADEMY, 21. Portrait of Procurator.

Woburn Abbey. 16. Portrait of Venetian Senator.

FRANCESCO BECCARUZZI.

Active in the second and third quarter of the XVI century. Pupil of Pordenone ; imitator of all his great Venetian contemporaries ; finally, imitator of Paul Veronese.

Belluno. 14. Woman in White Dress.
Bergamo. LOCHIS, 193. Portrait of Young Woman.
Berlin. HERR KAUFMANN, Portrait of Gentleman.
 HERR WESENDONCK, 10. Santa Conversazione.
Boston, U. S. A. 52. Copy of a (lost) Paris Bordone : Holy Family and Saints.
Buda-Pesth. 84. Bust of Woman.
 89. Madonna.
 109. Young Woman seated.
Cambridge. FITZWILLIAM MUSEUM, 138. Adoration of Shepherds.
Conegliano. DUOMO, R. WALL. Three Saints. E.
 S. M. DELLE GRAZIE, HIGH ALTAR, Madonna and Saints.
 S. ROCCO, ORGAN PICTURE, Madonna and Saints. L.
Dresden. 199. Calling of Matthew.
Ferrara. SALA II. Christ and the Adulteress.
Florence. UFFIZI, 585. Portrait of Man.
Glasgow. 29. Madonna enthroned with Saints and Angels.
Haigh Hall (near Wigan). LORD CRAWFORD, Bust of Woman.
Hopetoun House, N. B. LORD HOPETOUN, Gentleman with Horse and Groom.
Lille. 653. Stoning of Stephen (?)
 1056. Legend of Moses.
Linlathen, N. B. COL. ERSKINE, Bust of Man. Santa Conversazione.
London. BURLINGTON HOUSE, DIPLOMA GALLERY, Temperance.

London (*Con.*). APSLEY HOUSE, Portrait of Lady.
    MR. C. BUTLER, Portrait of Man. St. George and the Dragon.
    SIR WILLIAM FARRER, Santa Conversazione.
    DORCHESTER HOUSE, Portrait of Doge Andrea Gritti.
    VISCOUNT POWERSCOURT, Portrait of "Politian."
    LORD NORTHBROOK, Santa Conversazione.
    MR. G. SALTING, Portrait of Man.
Keir, N. B. MR. ARCHIBALD STIRLING, Young Woman playing Organ.
Milan. MUSEO CIVICO, 104. Portrait of Man with Spaniel.
Narbonne. 253. Marriage of St. Catherine.
Oldenburg. 81. Dead Christ.
Padua. 9. Santa Conversazione.
    1362. Bust of Monk in White.
Parma. 254. Portrait of Man.
Rome. COLONNA, 16. A Cavalier.
    DORIA, 62. Portrait of Woman. 386. Man with Flower.
Serravalle. S. ANTONIO, Baptism.
Strassburg. Scene taken from Lotto's Crucifixion at Monte San Giusto.
Stuttgart. 190. Bust of Man.
Toulouse. Holy Family and Infant John presenting Dove.
Treviso. MONTE DI PIETA, Dead Christ. Prophets.
    EREDI PERAZZOLO, Way to Golgotha.
    S. LUCIA, SACRISTY, St. Lucy.
Venice. ACADEMY, 517. St. Francis receiving Stigmata.
    525. Deposition.
    CORRER, Portrait of "Cesare Borgia."
    MANFRIN GALLERY. Santa Conversazione and Donor.
    QUIRINI-STAMPALIA, 68. Santa Conversazione.
    PALAZZO REALE, Madonna and St. Catherine.

THE VENETIAN PAINTERS. 89

Venice (*Con.*). GIOVANELLI, 315. St. Roch.
    S. M. DELL' ORTO, SS. Lawence, Helen, Gregory, Dominic, and Lorenzo Giustiniani.
Vienna. 157. Portrait of Lady.
    206. A Warrior.
    209. The Baptist.
    211. Thaddeus.
    ACADEMY, 5. St. Lawrence. 6. Nativity. 20. Deposition. 41. St. Paul.

GENTILE BELLINI.

1429–1507. Pupil of his father, Jacopo Bellini; influenced by the Paduans.

Buda-Pesth. 101. Portrait of Catherine Cornaro.
Frankfort a/M. 18. Bust of St. Mark. E.
London. 808. St. Peter Martyr.
    1213. Portrait of Mathematician.
    1440. Head of a Monk.
    MR. LUDWIG MOND, Madonna Enthroned. E.
Milan. BRERA, 168. Preaching of St. Mark. L. (Finished by Giovanni Bellini.)
Monopoli. DUOMO, St. Jerome and Donor (?). E.
Venice. ACADEMY, 570. Beato Lorenzo Giustiniani, 1465. 568. Miracle of True Cross, 1500. 567. Corpus Christi Procession, 1496. 563. Healing accomplished by Fragment of True Cross. L.
    MUSEO CORRER, Portrait of Doge Giovanni Mocenigo.
    SAN MARCO FABBRICERIA, ORGAN SHUTTERS, SS. Theodore and Mark, SS. Jerome and Francis. E.
    LADY LAYARD, Adoration of Magi. Portrait of Sultan Mohamet, 1480.

GIOVANNI BELLINI.

1430 (?)–1516. Pupil of his father, Jacopo; formed in Padua under the influence of Donatello.

Bergamo. LOCHIS, 210. Madonna. E.
MORELLI, 27. Madonna. 41. Madonna.
Berlin. 4. Pietà. L. 28. Dead Christ.
Florence. UFFIZI, 631. Allegory of Tree of Life. L.
London. 189. Portrait of Loredano. L. 280. Madonna. L. 726. Agony in Garden. E. 1233. Blood of Redeemer. E.
MR. LUDWIG MOND, Dead Christ. Madonna.
Milan. BRERA, 284. Pietà. E. 261. Madonna. 297. Madonna, 1510.
DR. GUST. FRIZZONI, Madonna. E.
Murano. S. PIETRO, Madonna with SS. Mark and Augustin and Doge Barbarigo, 1488.
Naples. SALA GRANDE, 7. Transfiguration.
Newport, U. S. A. MR. T. H. DAVIS, Madonna. E.
Pesaro. 11. Crucifixion (?). E. 52. God the Father.
S. FRANCESCO, Altar-piece in many parts.
Rimini. Dead Christ. E.
Turin. 779. Madonna. E.
Venice. ACADEMY, 596. Madonna. 594. Madonna. 595. Five small Allegories. L. 613. Madonna with St. Catherine and Magdalen. 610. Madonna with SS. Paul and George. 612. Madonna. 38. Madonna with six Saints.
MUSEO CORRER, SALA VII, 23. Transfiguration. E.
SALA IX, 27. Dead Christ. E. 46. Crucifixion. E.
54. Dead Christ supported by three Angels. E.
PALAZZO DUCALE, SALA DI TRÈ, Pietà. E.

Venice (Con.). FRARI, Triptych, Madonna and Saints, 1488.
    S. FRANCESCO DELLA VIGNA, Madonna and four Saints, 1507.
    S. GIOVANNI CRISOSTOMO, SS. Jerome, Augustin, and Christopher, 1513.
    S. MARIA DELL' ORTO, Madonna. E.
    S. ZACCARIA, Madonna and four Saints, 1505.
Verona. 77. Madonna. E.
Vicenza. S. CORONA, Baptism, 1510.

JACOPO BELLINI.

Active 1430–1470. Pupil of the Umbrian painter, Gentile da Fabriano, and of the Veronese, Pisanello.

Brescia. S. ALESSANDRO, Annunciation, with five Predelle.
Ferrara. SIG. VENDEGHINI, Adoration of Magi.
London. BRITISH MUSEUM, Sketch-Book. E.
Lovere. TADINI, Madonna.
Padua. SALA IV, Christ in Limbo.
Paris. Sketch-Book. L.
Venice. ACADEMY, 582. Madonna.
    MUSEO CORRER, SALA IX, 42. Crucifixion.
    S. TROVASO, S. Giovanni Crisogono on Horseback. (?)
Verona. 365. Christ on Cross.

BISSOLO.

1464–1528. Pupil and assistant of Giovanni Bellini.

Berlin. 43. Altar-piece. L.
Brescia. TOSIO, SALA XIV, 3. Madonna and Saints. E.
Chantilly. Madonna.
Düsseldorf. 75. Madonna with Infant John and his Parents.
Genoa. ANNUNZIATA, Madonna and four Saints.
Hampton Court. 117. Portrait of Man. E.

London.   MR. BENSON, Annunciation. Madonna.
           MR. MOND, Madonna with SS. Paul and
               Catherine.
Milan.   BRERA, 237. St. Stephen. 285. St. Antony of
               Padua. 298. A Bishop.
Rome.   VILLA BORGHESE, 176. Madonna. E.
Treviso.   DUOMO, Three Saints and Donor.
           S. ANDREA, Madonna and two Saints.
Venice.   ACADEMY, 88. Dead Christ. 93. Presentation
               in the Temple. 79. Christ Crowning S.
               Catherine. 94. Madonna with SS. James
               and Job.
           MUSEO CORRER, SALA IX, 57. Madonna with
               St. Peter Martyr.
           S. GIOVANNI IN BRAGORA, Triptych.
           S. MARIA MATER DOMINI, Transfiguration.
           REDENTORE, Madonna with SS. John and Cath-
               erine.
           LADY LAYARD, Madonna with SS. Michael and
               Ursula and Donors.
Verona.   Circumcision. E.
Vienna.   13. Lady at Toilet, 1515.
           4. Baptism.

BONIFAZIO VERONESE.

Active circa 1510–1540. Pupil of Palma Vecchio; influenced by Giorgione.

Bergamo. CARRARA, 197, 198. Small mythological Scenes.
             FRIZZONI-SALIS, Parable of Sower.
Boston, U. S. A. MRS. J. L. GARDNER, Santa Conver-
             sazione. E.
Campo S. Piero. ORATORY OF S. ANTONIO, Preaching
             of St. Antony (in part).
Dresden. 208. Finding of Moses.

Florence.	PITTI, 84. Madonna, St. Elizabeth, and Donor. E.
	89. Rest in Flight.
	161. Finding of Moses.
	405. Christ among the Doctors (in part).
Hague.	252. Bust of Woman.
Hampton Court.	146. Santa Conversazione.
Lille.	717. Esther before Ahasuerus.
London.	1202. Santa Conversazione. E.
	MR. BENSON, Allegories of Morning, and of Night (in part).
	Mr. BUTLER, Santa Conversazione. Rape of Helen. Subject from a Romance.
	MR. CHARLES T. D. CREWS, Birth of John.
	DR. RICHTER, Joseph drawn out of the Well. Head of Pompey brought to Cæsar.
Milan.	BRERA, 209. Finding of Moses.
	AMBROSIANA, 231. Holy Family with Tobias and Angel. E.
	POLDI-PEZZOLI, PINACOTECA, 99. Doctor Visiting a Patient.
Paris.	1171. Santa Conversazione.
Rome.	VILLA BORGHESE, 156. Mother of Zebedee's Children. 186. Return of the Prodigal Son.
	COLONNA, 1. Holy Family with SS. Jerome and Lucy.
	DORIA, 16. Santa Conversazione.
	PRINCE CHIGI, Finding of Moses.
Venice.	ACADEMY, 291. Rich Man's Feast. 319. Massacre of Innocents. 295. Judgment of Solomon, 1533 (in part).
	PALAZZO REALE, Madonna with SS. Catherine and John the Almsgiver, 1533.
	GIOVANELLI, Santa Conversazione.
	LADY LAYARD, Twelve very small pictures: Rustic Occupations.

Vienna. 193. Santa Conversazione.
201. Triumph of Love. 156. Triumph of Chastity.
145. Salome.

FRANCESCO BONSIGNORI.

1453 (?)–1519. Pupil of Bartolommeo and Alvise Vivarini; influenced by Giovanni Bellini, and later by Mantegna and his own townsman, Liberale of Verona.

Bergamo. LOCHIS, 154. Portrait of a Gonzaga.
MORELLI, 45. The Widow's Son. L.
Berlin. 46ᶜ. St. Sebastian.
Florence. BARGELLO, Christ bearing Cross. L.
Fonthill (Wilts). MR. ALFRED MORRISON, Portrait of Man.
Gosford House, N. B. LORD WEMYS, Madonna enthroned.
London. 736. Portrait of Man, 1487.
Mantua. ACCADEMIA VIRGILIANA, Way to Golgotha. Vision of the Nun Osanna.
Milan. BRERA, 163. St. Bernardino. 170. SS. Bernardino and Louis holding the Initials of Christ.
POLDI-PEZZOLI, Head of a female Saint. St. Bernardino. Profile of Old Man. Bust of Venetian Noble.
Paris. PRINCE SCIARRA, Bust of a Gonzaga.
Venice. PALAZZO DUCALE, DIRECTORS' ROOM. Madonna. E.
S. GIOVANNI E PAOLO, 2d Altar R. Altar-piece in 9 parts. E.
Verona. 148. Madonna, 1483. 271. Madonna enthroned with four Saints, 1484.
S. BERNARDINO, Madonna enthroned with SS. Jerome and George, 1488.
S. NAZZARO E CELSO, Madonna and Saints, finished by Girolamo dai Libri.
S. PAOLO, Madonna with St. Antony Abbot and the Magdalen. E.

PARIS BORDONE.

1495-1570. Pupil and follower of Titian; influenced later by Michelangelo.

Ashridge. LORD BROWNLOW, Apollo and the Muses.
Bergamo. LOCHIS, 41, 42. Vintage Scenes.
Berlin. 169. Chess Players.
         191. Madonna and four Saints.
Chatsworth. DUKE OF DEVONSHIRE, Family Group.
Cologne. 811$^{A.A.}$ Bathsheba.
Dresden. 203. Apollo and Marsyas.
         204. Diana as Huntress.
         205. Holy Family and St. Jerome.
Edinburgh. 506. Lady at her Toilet.
Florence. PITTI, 109. Portrait of Woman.
         UFFIZI, 607. Portrait of Young Man.
Genoa. BRIGNOLE-SALE, SALA V. Portrait of Man.
         SALA VIII, Santa Conversazione. Portrait of Man.
Glasgow. 45. Holy Family.
         46. Holy Family. E.
Gosford House, N. B. LORD WEMYS, A Courtesan.
Hampton Court. 118. Madonna with male and female Donors.
Keir, N. B. MR. ARCHIBALD STIRLING, Madonna and Infant John.
London. 637. Daphnis and Chloe.
         674. Portrait of Lady.
         BRIDGEWATER HOUSE, Holy Family.
         LORD BROWNLOW, Cavalier in Armour.
         THE MISSES COHEN, Portrait of a Lady seated.
         MR. G. DONALDSON, A Courtesan.
         DR. RICHTER, Christ among the Doctors.
         LORD ROSEBERY, Portrait of a Lady.
Lovere. TADINI, Madonna with SS. George and Christopher.

Milan.	BRERA, 212. Baptism. 216. Descent of Holy Spirit.
241. S. Dominic presented to Saviour by Virgin.
242. Madonna and Saints.
306 bis. Three Heads.
St. Ambrose presenting a General to Virgin.
SIGNOR CRESPI, Jove and a Nymph.
S. MARIA PRESSO CELSO, Madonna and St. Jerome.
Munich.	1121. Man counting Jewels.
New York,	U. S. A. HISTORICAL SOCIETY, 205. Rest in Flight.
Padua.	SALA EMO, 93. Christ taking leave of his Mother.
Paris.	1178. Portrait of Man. 1179. Portrait of Man, 1540.
Richmond.	SIR F. COOK, Hunting Piece.
Rome.	VILLA BORGHESE, 119. Jupiter and Antiope.
COLONNA, 92. Holy Family with St. Jerome. 116. Holy Family, SS. Sebastian, and Jerome.
DORIA, 294. Venus and Mars.
VATICAN, ANTE-CHAMBER OF POPE'S APARTMENTS, St. George and the Dragon.
Siena.	SALA IX, 9. Annunciation. 51. Madonna and Donor.
Strassburg.	Madonna and St. Jerome.
Treviso.	4. Madonna with SS. Jerome and John the Baptist.
DUOMO, Adoration of Shepherds. Madonna with SS. Sebastian and Jerome. Gospel Scenes (on a small picture).
Venice.	ACADEMY, 320. Fisherman and Doge. E. 322. Paradise.
PALAZZO DUCALE, CHAPEL, Dead Christ.
GIOVANELLI, Madonna and Saints.

Venice (*Con.*). LADY LAYARD, Christ baptising a Youth
 in Prison.
 S. GIOVANNI IN BRAGORA, Last Supper.
 S. GIOBBE, S. Andrew and two other Saints.
Vienna. 233. Allegory.
 246. Allegory.
 248. Lady at Toilet.
 231. Young Woman.
 CZERNIN, Venetian adoring Cross.

ANTONIO CANALE called CANALETTO.
1697-1768.

Biel, N. B. MRS. HAMILTON OGILVIE, View of Scalzi.
Buda-Pesth. 659. The Pantheon.
Dresden. 581. The Grand Canal.
 582. S. Giovanni e Paolo.
 583. Campo S. Giacomo di Rialto.
 584. Piazza di S. Marco.
Florence. UFFIZI, 1064. The Piazzetta.
Frankfort a/M. 51. Entrance to Grand Canal.
 53. Venetian Palace and Bridge.
Hampton Court. The Colosseum, 1753.
Hopetoun House, N. B. LORD HOPETOUN, Venice from Lagoon.
London. 127. Scuola della Carità. 937. Scuola di San Rocco.
 THE MISSES COHEN, Three Studies.
 DORCHESTER HOUSE, View of Piazzetta from Lagoon.
 HERTFORD HOUSE, Thirteen views of Venice.
 MR. MOND, Two views of the Piazza.
 DR. RICHTER, The Dogana.
 DUKE OF WESTMINSTER, Grand Canal.
Milan. CASA SORMANI, The Bucentaur. Reception of an Ambassador.

New Battle, N. B. MARQUIS OF LOTHIAN, St. Paul's from the Thames. S. Giorgio Maggiore.
Paris. 1203. The Salute.
MME. ANDRÉ, Two views of Venice.
M. MAURICE KANN, Salute. Pescheria.
Vienna. LICHTENSTEIN, 191, 192, 193, 196, 198, 199, 203, 204, 205, 206, 210, 216, 217. Views of Venice.
Windsor Castle. Series of large views of the Piazza.
Woburn Abbey. Twenty-four views of Venice.

DOMENICO CAPRIOLI.

Active 1518–circa 1560. Influenced by Titian, Paris Bordone, Pordenone, Bonifazio, Savoldo, and Moretto.

Berlin. 156. Portrait of Man in Black.
158. Tennis Player and Page. L.
195. St. Sebastian.
Brighton. MR. H. WILLETT, Madonna of Mercy.
Cambridge, U. S. A. PROF. C. E. NORTON, Portrait of Domenico Grimani.
Castle Barnard. BOWES MUSEUM, 339. Portrait of Man, 1528.
Dijon. 6. Assumption.
London. LORD ASHBURNHAM, Portrait of Titian. L.
MR. R. BENSON, Madonna in Profile (?). E.
DUKE OF GRAFTON, Portrait of Man. 1541.
Motta Di Livenza. S. M. DEI MIRACOLI, Adoration of Shepherds.
Naples. MUSEO FILANGIERI, 1438. Entombment. L.
New Battle, N. B. MARQUIS OF LOTHIAN, Return of Prodigal.
Paris. MME. C. DE ROSENBERG, Portrait of Doge Grimani.
Rome. BORGHESE, 130, 132. Caricatured Heads.
COLONNA, 12. Portrait of Sciarra Colonna.

Treviso.   50. Nativity. 1518.
Vienna.   212. Young Hero.
           ACADEMY, 508. Picnic.   510. Country Dance.
Windsor.   Portrait of Domenico Grimani.

GIOVANNI BUSI, called CARIANI.

Circa 1480-1544. Pupil of Giovanni Bellini and Palma; influenced by Giorgione and Capaccio.

Ashridge.   LORD BROWNLOW, Bust of Bart. Colleoni.
Basel.   166. Bust of Young Man.
Bergamo.   CARRARA, 67. Madonna with SS. Helen, Constantine, and other Saints. L. 85. Portrait of Lady. 135. Bust of Man.
   LOCHIS, 2. Portrait of Lady. 85. Christ on Cross, bust of Donor, 1518. 146. Woman playing, and Shepherd asleep. 150. St. Antony of Padua. E. 153. Portrait of Monk. 165. Portrait of Man. 172. Christ bearing Cross. E. 184. Portrait of Bened. Caravaggio. 192. St. Stephen. 182. Small St. Jerome. 196. St. Catherine.
   MORELLI, Madonna. L. Portrait of Man.
   DUOMO, Back of High Altar, Madonna. E.
   BAGLIONI, Madonna and Donor, 1520.
   SIGNOR FRIZZONI-SALIS, Madonna and Saints. L.
   PICCINELLI, Flight into Egypt. L.
   RONCALLI, Family Group, 1519.
   COUNT SUARDI, St. Jerome. Portrait of Senator.
Berlin.   185. Girl in Landscape. 188. Portrait of Man.
Buda-Pesth.   79. Madonna and St. Francis.
Chatsworth.   DUKE OF DEVONSHIRE, Portrait of Young Man.
Glasgow.   142. Christ and the Adulteress.

Hampton Court.   135. Adoration of Shepherds.   L.
                    Venus. L.
London.   41. Death of St. Peter Martyr. L. 1203.
                    Madonna and Saints. L.
                    SOUTH KENSINGTON, Venus and Mars (lent).
                    MR. BENSON, Madonna and Donors. Portrait
                    of Man wearing Sword.
                    MR. DOETSCH, Nativity,
                    DORCHESTER HOUSE, Portrait of Man.
                    MARQUIS OF LANSDOWNE, A Concert.
                    MR. SALTING, Portrait of Senator.
Marseilles. St. Sebastian with St. Roch and a female Saint.
Milan.   BRERA, 210. Madonna and Saints. L. 291.
                    Madonna. L.
                    MUSEO CIVICO, 106. Lot and his Daughters.
                    COLLECTION DELL' ACQUA. Portrait of a Lady.
                    AMBROSIANA, Way to Golgotha.
                    BORROMEO, Nativity. St. Jerome.
                    POLDI-PEZZOLI, 133. Madonna and Saints.
                    BONOMI-CEREDA, Portrait of Man. Magdalen.
Munich.   1107. Portrait of Man.
                    LOTZBECK COLLECTION, 100. Portrait of Man.
New York, U. S. A. HISTORICAL SOCIETY, 206. Portrait
                    of Man.
Oldenburg. 78. Holy Family and Saints.
                    82. Two Women and a Man.
Paris.   1135. Madonna, Saints, and Donor. E.
                    1156. Two Men.
                    1159. Holy Family with SS. Sebastian and
                    Catherine.
                    M. AYNARD, Portrait of Man.
Rome.   VILLA BORGHESE, 30. Sleeping Venus. 164.
                    Madonna and St. Peter. 311. Woman
                    with three Men.
                    CORSINI. Santa Conversazione.
                    VATICAN. Bust of Doge.

St. Petersburg. 116. Young Woman and old Man.
Strassburg. 69. Young Man playing Guitar. Portrait of old Venetian.
Stuttgart. 36. Portrait of a Lady.
Venice. ACADEMY, 300. Portrait of Man, 1526. 326. Holy Family. 299. Portrait of Man. 272. Bust of Old Woman.
Vicenza. SALA. II, 41. Madonna and Saints.
Vienna. 63. St. Sebastian. 60. Christ bearing Cross. 207. The " Bravo." 205. St. John Evangelist. ACADEMY, 77. Madonna with SS. John and Catherine.
Zogno. CHURCH, Adoration of Shepherds.

VITTORE CARPACCIO.

Active 1478–1522. Pupil and follower of Gentile Bellini.
Berlin. 14. Madonna with SS. Catherine and Jerome. E. 23. Consecration of Stephen, 1511.
Caen. 171. Santa Conversazione (in part). L.
Ferrara. SALA VIII, 10. Death of the Virgin, 1508.
Florence. UFFIZI, 583 *bis*. Fragment, Finding of True Cross.
Frankfort a/M. 38. Madonna and Infant John.
Haigh Hall (near Wigan). LORD CRAWFORD, Portrait of Lady.
London. 750. Madonna with SS. John and Christopher, and Doge Giovanni Mocenigo, 1478.
Mr. BENSON, Female Saint Reading.
Milan. BRERA, 288. Stephen disputing, 1514. 307. Presentation of Virgin (in part). L. 309. Marriage of Virgin (in part). L.
Paris. 1211. Stephen preaching. L.
Stuttgart. 13. Glory of St. Thomas, 1507.
122. Martyrdom of Stephen, 1515.

Venice. ACADEMY, 89. Martyrdom of the 10,000 Virgins, 1515. 566. Healing of Madman in view of Rialto, 1494. 572, 573, 574, 575, 1495; 579, 1490; 577, 578, 580, 1493; 576, 1491. Story of St. Ursula. 90. Meeting of Joachim and Anna, 1515. 44. Presentation of Infant Christ, 1510.
MUSEO CORRER, SALA IX, 14. Visitation. L. SALA X, 8. Two Courtesans.
PALAZZO DUCALE, SALA DI TRÈ, Lion of S. Marco, 1516.
S. GIORGIO MAGGIORE, SALA DEL CONCLAVE, St. George and the Dragon, with predellé, 1512.
S. GIORGIO DEGLI SCHIAVONI, ten pictures along walls of Oratory on ground floor, and Madonna over altar. St. George slaying Dragon; St. George bringing Dragon captive; St. George baptising the Princess and her Father, MDV. . . ; Story of St. Tryphonius; Agony in Garden; Christ in House of Pharisee, 1502; St. Jerome bringing his Lion to Monastery; Burial of St. Jerome, 1502; St. Jerome in his Study.
S. VITALE, St. Vitale between SS. George and Valeria, 1514.
LADY LAYARD, Augustus aud Sibyl. L. Death and Assumption of Virgin. L. St. Ursula taking leave of her Father.

Vienna. 7. Christ adored by Angels, 1496.

VINCENZO CATENA.

Active 1495–1531. Pupil of the Bellini; influenced by Carpaccio and Giorgione.

Ashridge. LORD BROWNLOW, Nativity.

THE VENETIAN PAINTERS. 103

Bergamo. CARRARA, 11. Christ at Emaus.
Berlin. 32. Portrait of Fugger. L. 19. Madonna, Saints, and Donor. E. 4. Pietà.
NAZIONAL GALERIE, RACZYNSKI COLLECTION. 13. Madonna and Saints. E.
Boston, U. S. A. MRS. J. L. GARDNER, Christ giving Keys to Peter.
Buda-Pesth. 74. Madonna, Saints, and Donor. E.
76. Bust of female Saint.
78. Holy Family and female Saint. E.
Cologne. 730ᴱ. Madonna.
Dresden. 65. Holy Family. L. 54. Madonna and two Saints. E.
Glasgow. 73. Madonna with St. Catherine and the Magdalen.
Liverpool. 81. Madonna with four Saints and Donor. E.
London. 234. Warrior adoring Infant Christ. L.
694. St. Jerome in his Study. L.
1121. Bust of youth.
1160. Adoration of Magi. L.
1455. Circumcision.
LORD ASHBURNHAM, Madonna, two Saints, and Donor, 1505.
MR. BENSON, Holy Family. L.
MR. BEAUMONT, Nativity. (?)
MR. C. BUTLER, Christ at the Well. L.
MR. HESELTINE, Madonna.
MR. MOND, Madonna, Saints, and Donor. E.
Modena. 404. Madonna and two Saints.
Nimes. 174. Head of an Apostle.
Padua. SALA EMO, 29. Circumcision. E.
Paris. 1157. Reception of Venetian Ambassadors at Cairo.
MME. ANDRÉ, Portrait of Woman.
M. LÉOPOLD GOLDSCHMIDT, Bust of Woman.
M. SALOMON GOLDSCHMIDT, Circumcision.

Rome.	DORIA, 326. Circumcision.
Venice.	PALAZZO DUCALE, SALA DI TRÈ, Madonna, two Saints, and Doge Loredan. E.
	QUIRINI-STAMPALIA, SALA III, 1. Judith. L.
	GIOVANELLI, Madonna with John the Baptist and female Saint. E.
	S. MARIA MATER DOMINI, St. Christina.
	S. SIMEON PROFETA, The Trinity. E.
	S. TROVASO, Madonna. E.
Vienna.	20. Portrait of a Canon.

GIOVANNI BATTISTA CIMA.

1460–1517 circa. Pupil of Alvise Vivarini; influenced by Giovanni Bellini.

Ashridge. LORD BROWNLOW, Small Holy Family and Saints.
Bergamo. MORELLI, 57. Madonna.
Berlin. 2. Madonna enthroned with four Saints.
    7. Madonna and Donor.
    15. Healing of Anianus (in part).
    17. Madonna.
Bologna. 61. Madonna.
Boston, U. S. A. MR. QUINCY SHAW, Madonna. E.
Conegliano. DUOMO, Madonna and Saints, 1493.
Dresden. 61. The Saviour. 63. Presentation of Virgin.
Düsseldorf. 18. Madonna. Coronation (in part). L.
Frankfort a/M. 39. Madonna.
    40. Madonna and two Saints,
London. 300. Madonna. 634. Madonna. 816. Incredulity of Thomas, 1504. 1120. St. Jerome. 1310. Ecce Homo. (?)
    HERTFORD HOUSE, St. Catherine.
    MR. LUDWIG MOND, Two Saints.
    MR. J. E. TAYLOR, Madonna with two Saints (lunette).

Milan.	BRERA, 191. SS. Peter Martyr, Augustin, and Nicholas of Bari. 286. SS. Jerome, Nicholas of Tolentino, Ursula, and another female Saint. 289. SS. Luke, Mary, John the Baptist, and Mark. 293. Madonna. 300. St. Peter between John the Baptist and St. Paul, 1516. 302. St. Jerome. 303. St. Giustina and two other Saints. POLDI-PEZZOLI, Head of Female Saint.
Modena.	143. Pietà.
Munich.	1033. Madonna with Mary Magdalen and St. Jerome. E.
Olera.	CHURCH, Polyptych. E.
Parma.	360. Madonna with SS. Cosmos and Damian. 361. Madonna with SS. Michael and Augustin. 370. Endymion. 373. Apollo and Marsyas.
Paris.	1259. Madonna with John and Magdalen.
Richmond.	SIR F. COOK, Madonna.
Venice.	ACADEMY, 603. Madonna with SS. John and Paul. 604. Pietà. 597. Madonna. 611. Christ, Thomas, and Magnus. 36. Madonna with six Saints. 592. Tobias and Angel, SS. James and Nicholas. SEMINARIO, God, the Father (small lunette). CARMINE, Adoration of Shepherds. S. GIOVANNI IN BRAGORA, Baptism, 1494. SS. Helen and Constantine. Three Predelle with Story of Finding of True Cross. S. GIOVANNI E PAOLO, Coronation of the Virgin. S. MARIA DELL' ORTO, St. John between SS. Paul, Jerome, Mark, and Peter. LADY LAYARD, Madonna with SS. Francis and Paul. Madonna with SS. Nicholas of Bari and John the Baptist.

Vicenza. SALA IV, 18. Madonna with SS. Jerome and John, 1489.
Vienna. 19. Madonna with SS. Jerome and Louis.

CARLO CRIVELLI.

B. 1430–40; d. after 1493. Pupil of the first Vivarini; influenced by the Paduans.

Ancona. 1. Madonna. E.
Ascoli. DUOMO, Altar-piece, with Pietà, 1473.
Bergamo. LOCHIS, 129. Madonna.
Berlin. 1156. The Magdalen.
1156A. Madonna, St. Peter and six other Saints.
Brussels. 16. Madonna. 17. St. Francis.
Buda-Pesth. Madonna.
Florence. PANCIATICHI, 101. Pietà, 1485.
Frankfort a/M. 33, 34. Annunciation.
London. 602. Pietà.
668. The Blessed Ferretti in Ecstasy.
724. Madonna with SS. Sebastian and Jerome.
739. Annunciation, 1486.
788. Altar-piece in thirteen compartments, 1476.
809. Madonna with SS. Sebastian and Francis, 1491.
906. Madonna in Ecstasy, 1492.
907. SS. Catherine and Magdalen.
LADY ASHBURTON, St. Dominic. St. George.
MR. BENSON, Madonna, 1472.
MR. R. CRAWSHAY, Pietà.
HERTFORD HOUSE, St. Roch.
MR. MOND, SS. Peter and Paul.
LORD NORTHBROOK, Madonna. E. Resurrection. E. SS. Bernardino and Catherine.
MR. STUART M. SAMUEL, St. George and the Dragon.
SOUTH KENSINGTON, JONES COLLECTION, 665. Madonna.

Macerata. 36. Madonna, 1470.
Massa
  Fermana. MUNICIPIO, Altar-piece, 1468.
Milan.   BRERA, 189. Crucifixion. 193. Madonna. L.
       283. Madonna and Saints, 1482. 294. SS.
       James, Bernardino, and Pellegrino. 295.
       SS. Antony Abbot, Jerome, and Andrew.
       GALLERIA OGGIONO, Coronation of Virgin,
       with John, Catherine, Francis, Augustin,
       and other Saints (in great part). Above, a
       Pietà, 1493.
       MUSEO CIVICO, COLLECTION DELL' ACQUA, St.
       John. St. Bartholomew.
       POLDI-PEZZOLI, SALA DORATA, 20. St. Francis
       adoring Christ. PINACOTECA, 78. St. Sebastian.
Paris.   1268. St. Bernardino, 1477.
Pausula. S. AGOSTINO, Madonna.
Richmond. SIR F. COOK, Madonna. E.
Rome.   LATERAN, Madonna, 1482.
       VATICAN, Pietà.
Strassburg. Adoration of Shepherds.
Venice.   ACADEMY, 103. SS. Jerome and Augustin.
       SS. Peter and Paul.
Verona.   351. Madonna. E.

GIORGIONE.

1478-1510. Pupil of Giovanni Bellini; influenced by Carpaccio.

Berlin.   12ᴬ. Portrait of Man. E.
Buda-Pesth. 94. Portrait of Antonio Brocardo.
Castelfranco. DUOMO, Madonna with SS. Francis and Liberale. E.
Dresden.   185. Sleeping Venus.

Florence. UFFIZI, 621. Trial of Moses. E.
622. Knight of Malta.
630. Judgment of Solomon. E.
Hampton Court. 101. Shepherd with Pipe.
Madrid. Madonna with SS. Roch and Antony of Padua.
Paris. 1136. Fête Champêtre.
Rome. VILLA BORGHESE, 143. Portrait of a Lady.
Venice. ACADEMY, 516. Storm calmed by St. Mark.
L. Finished, in small part, by Paris Bordone.
SEMINARIO, Apollo and Daphne.
GIOVANELLI, Gipsy and Soldier.
S. ROCCO, Christ bearing Cross.
Vicenza. CASA LOSCHI, Christ bearing Cross. E.
Vienna. 16. Evander showing Æneas the Site of Rome.

GUARDI.

1712–1793. Pupil of Canaletto.

Albi. 1. View of Salute and Giudecca.
Amiens. 216, 217, 219. Views.
Badger Hall (Shropshire). MR. F. CAPEL-CURE, Scuola di San Marco.
Bassano. SALA DEL CAVALLO, 85. The Piazza.
Bergamo. LOCHIS, 89–93, 106–108. Landscapes and Views.
SIGNOR BAGLIONI, Two Venetian Views.
COUNT MORONI, Villa by the Sea.
Berlin. 501^A. Grand Canal. 501^B. Lagoon. 501$^{C\ \&\ D}$. Cemetery Island.
Biel, N. B. MRS. HAMILTON OGILVIE, Salute. Redentore.
Boston, U. S. A. MRS. J. L. GARDNER, Large view of Venice.
Brighton. MR. CONSTANTINE IONDES, Piazza in Mist.
Brussels. 280. Scene in St. Mark's.
Buda-Pesth. 629–640. Views of Venice.
Cambridge. FITZWILLIAM MUSEUM, Four small views.
Edinburgh. 600, 602. Landscapes.

Glasgow.   202, 203.   Views of Venice.
Hamburg.   CONSUL WEBER, 143. Ruins.   144. Rialto.
London.   210, 1054.   Views in Venice.
           SOUTH KENSINGTON, JONES COLLECTION, 104.
             View near Venice.
           THE MISSES COHEN, Three Studies.
           DORCHESTER HOUSE, View from Piazzetta.
           SIR WM. FARRER, View near Venice.
           SIR A. WOLLASTON FRANKS, An Island.
           SIR JULIAN GOLDSCHMID, Boat Race.
           HERTFORD HOUSE, Nine Views of Venice.
           LORD HOUGHTON, View of Riva.
           MR. MOND, Pius VI holding a Reception.
           DR. RICHTER, Cannareggio.
           MR. SALTING, The Rialto.   View near Venice.
             Gothic Ruins.   Classic Ruins.
           MRS. ANDERSON WESTON, Grand Canal.
Milan.   MUSEO CIVICO, 69, 71-74.   Landscapes.
           POLDI-PEZZOLI, 87. Piazetta. 89. Dogana.
             116, 117.   Tiny Landscapes.
           SIGNOR BERTINI, View of Lagoon.
           PRINCE TRIVULZIO, Two small Landscapes.
Modena.   143. Piazzetta.
           180. S. Giorgio.
Montpellier. 483. Storm on Canal.
Naples.   MUSEO FILANGIERI, Court of Doge's Palace.
New York, U.S.A. METROPOLITAN MUSEUM. 2. Salute.
             6. Rialte.
Oxford.   TAYLORIAN MUSEUM, 65, 66.   Views in Venice.
Padua.   300, 381. Views in Venice. 802. Hunting Scene.
Paris.   211. Procession of Doge to S. Zaccaria.
           1328. Embarkment in Bucentaur. 1329. Fes-
             tival at Salute.
           1330. " Jeudi Gras à Venise." 1331. Corpus
             Christi.
           1333. Sala di Collegio. 1334. Coronation of Doge.

Paris (*Con.*). MME. ANDRÉ, Two Views of Venice.
M. LÉOPOLD GOLDSCHMIDT, Dogana. Piazzetta.
Richmond. SIR F. COOK, The Piazza.
Rome. COLONNA, 78. Venetian Church.
DON MARCELLO MASSARENTI, Doge's Palace.
Rouen. 235. A Villa.
Strassburg. 18. The Rialto.
Toulouse. 2. Rialto. E.
22. Bucentaur. E.
Turin. 290 *bis*. Cottage. 781. Staircase. 782. Bridge over Canal.
Venice. MUSEO CORRER, SALA X, 25. The Ridotto. 26. Parlour of Convent of S. Zaccaria.
Verona. 223, 225. Landscapes.

BERNARDINO LICINIO.

Active 1520-1544. Pupil of Pordenone; influenced by Giorgione, Palma, and Bonifazio.

Alnwick. DUKE OF NORTHUMBERLAND, Family Group.
Balcarres, N. B. LORD CRAWFORD, Portrait of Man. 1535.
Bergamo. LOCHIS, 197. Portrait of a Lady.
SIGNOR PICCINELLI, Madonna and Saints.
Berlin. 198. Portrait of Young Woman.
Boston, U. S. A. MR. QUINCY SHAW, Madonna and two Saints.
Brescia. MARTINENGO, SALA C, 16. Portrait of a Young Man, 1520.
DUOMO VECCHIO, Christ bearing Cross. Adoration of Shepherds.
Brighton. MR. H. WILLETT, Board of a Harpsichord.
Buda-Pesth. 91. Portrait of Lady.
HERR RATH, Portrait of Lady.

THE VENETIAN PAINTERS.   111

Cambridge, U. S. A.   PROF. C. E. NORTON, Portrait of Young Man.
Dresden.   200. Portrait of a Lady, 1533.
Florence.   UFFIZI, 574. Madonna with St. Francis. 587. Portrait of Man.
Genoa.   BRIGNOLE-SALE, SALA VII, Portrait of Francesco Philetus.
Hampton Court. 71. Lady playing on Virginals. 104. Family Group, 1524.
London.   Portrait of a Young Man.
    LADY ASHBURTON, Young Man with his Hand on a Skull.
    MR. C. BUTLER, Portrait of Lady, 1522.
    MR. DOETSCH, Barbara Kressin, 1544.
    DORCHESTER HOUSE, Portrait of Man. Adoration of Shepherds.
Lucca.   SALA I, 68. Santa Conversazione.
Milan.   MUSEO CIVICO, 88. Portrait of Lady.
    ARCHBISHOP'S PALACE, Holy Family.
    SIGNOR CRESPI, Santa Conversazione.
    CASA SCOTTI, Holy Family with two Shepherds. Madonna, three Saints, male and female Donors.
Modena.   123. Portrait of a Lady.
Munich.   1120. Portrait of Man, 1523.
Münster in W.   143. Bust of Man, 1530.
Padua.   SALA ROMANINO, 814. Portrait of Young Man.
Rome.   VILLA BORGHESE, 115. Family Group. 171. Santa Conversazione.
    MISS HERTZ, Head of Ceres.
Rossie Priory, N. B.   LORD KINNAIRD, Portrait of Lady.
Rovigo.   4. St. Margaret between SS. Catherine and Lucy. 8. Portrait of a Scholar.
Saletto.   CHURCH, St. Silvester between S. Antony of Padua and Giustina, 1535.
Venice.   303. Portrait of Woman.

Venice (*Con.*). 311. Group of Putti.
        304. Portrait of Young Woman.
        LADY LAYARD, Santa Conversazione.
        FRARI, Madonna enthroned with Saints.
        The predella contains five Friars.
Vienna. 22. Portrait of Ottaviano Grimani, 1541.
        HARRACH COLLECTION, Madonna and female Donor.

PIETRO LONGHI.

1702–1762. Follower of the Bolognese painter, Crespi.

Bergamo. LOCHIS, 60. Gambling Scene. 61. Coffee Scene.
        MORELLI, 94. Portrait of Girl.
        SIG. BAGLIONI, Country Party.
Cambridge, U. S. A. PROF. C. E. NORTON. Portrait of Senator.
Dresden. 595. Portrait of Lady.
Florence. MR. LOESER, Milliner Scene.
Hampton Court. 549, 551. Genre pictures, 1744.
Keir, N. B. MR. ARCH. STIRLING, Lady sitting for Portrait.
London. 1100, 1101. Genre pictures. 1102. Andrea Tron.
        MR. F. CAVENDISH-BENTINCK, Visit to Nuns.
        MR. ARTHUR JAMES, Four genre pictures.
        MR. MOND, Card Party. Portrait of a Lady.
        DR. RICHTER, Card Party. Lady at Toilet.
Milan. SIGNOR CRESPI, Portrait of Man.
Modena. 215. A Letter Writer.
Venice. ACADEMY, 464–470. Genre pictures.
        MUSEO CORRER, SALA X, 25, 26, 31–40. Scenes of Venetian Life. 41. Boys on Horseback. Portrait of Goldoni.

THE VENETIAN PAINTERS.   113

Venice (Con.). PALAZZO GRASSI, STAIRCASE, Frescoes: Seven
  Scenes of Fashionable Life.
  QUIRINI-STAMPALIA, SALA X, 220. Portrait of
    Daniele Dolfino.
    SALA XIII, 11–17. The Seven Sacraments.
    18. Temptation of St. Antony. 19. Gam-
    bling Scene. 20. A Circus. 21. Monks
    and Canons. 22. Study of Geography.
    26, 299. Portraits of Ladies.

LORENZO LOTTO.

1480–1556. Pupil of Alvise Vivarini; influenced by Giovanni
  Bellini and Giorgione.

Alzano Maggiore (near Bergamo).   DUOMO, Assassination
  of St. Peter Martyr.
Ancona.   13. Assumption of Virgin, 1550. 37. Madonna
  with four Saints. L.
Asolo.   Madonna in Glory with two Saints, 1506.
Bergamo.   CARRARA, Three Predelle belonging to S. Bar-
  tolommeo Altar-piece. 66. Marriage of S.
  Catherine, with portrait of N. Bonghi, 1523.
  Portrait of a Lady.
  LOCHIS, 32, 33, 34. Sketches for Predelle, con-
  taining the story of S. Stephen. 185. Holy
  Family and S. Catherine, 1533.
  S. ALESSANDRO IN COLONNA, Pietà.
  S. ALESSANDRO IN CROCE, Trinity.
  S. BARTOLOMMEO, Altar-piece, 1516.
  S. BERNARDINO, Altar-piece, 1521.
  S. MARIA MAGGIORE, Intarsias, 1524–1530.
  S. MICHELE, Frescoes in Chapel L. of Choir.
  S. SPIRITO, Altar-piece, 1521.
  SIGNOR PICCINELLI, Madonna with SS. Sebas-
  tian and Roch.

Berlin.   153. Portrait of an Architect.
          182, 320. Portraits of Young Men.
          323. SS. Sebastian and Christopher, 1531.
          325. Christ taking leave of his Mother, 1522.
Brescia. TOSIO, SALA XIII, 34. Nativity.
Buda-Pesth. Angel with Globe and Sceptre (originally top of S. Bartolommeo Altar-piece at Bergamo).
Celana (near Bergamo). CHURCH, Assumption of Virgin, 1527.
Cingoli (Province of Macerata). S. DOMENICO, Madonna with six Saints, and fifteen small scenes from the Lives of Christ and the Virgin, 1539.
Costa di Mezzate (near Bergamo). Marriage of St. Catherine, 1522.
Dresden. 295. Madonna, 1518.
Florence. UFFIZI, 575. Holy Family with St. Jerome, 1534.
Hamburg. CONSUL WEBER, 33. St. Jerome.
Hampton Court. 114. Portrait of Young Man. E.
          148. Portrait of Andrea Odoni, 1527.
Hermannstadt. St. Jerome.
Jesi.[1] MUNICIPIO, Three Predelle containing Story of St. Lucy.
          LIBRARY, Pietà, 1512.
          Annunciation. St. Lucy before the Judge. Madonna and Saints, Francis receiving Stigmata (lunette) 1526. Visitation, Annunciation (lunette) 1530.
London.   699. Portraits of Agostino and Niccolo della Torre, 1515.
          1047. Family Group.
          1105. Portrait of Prothonotary Giuliano.
          BRIDGEWATER HOUSE, Madonna and Saints. E.

---

[1] All the Lottos at Jesi are presently to be transported to th Palazzo della Signoria.

THE VENETIAN PAINTERS. 115

London (*Con.*). DORCHESTER HOUSE, Portrait of a Lady.
MRS. MARTIN COLNAGHI, Madonna with SS. Jerome and Antony of Padua, 1522.
SIR W. M. CONWAY, Danäe. E.

Loreto. PALAZZO APOSTOLICO, 30. SS. Christopher, Sebastian, and Roch. 34. Christ and Adulteress. 42. Nativity. 25, 27. SS. Lucy and Thecla. 24, 28. Two Prophets. L. 31. Michael driving Lucifer from Heaven. L. 32. Presentation in Temple. L. 21. Baptism. L. 20. Adoration of Magi. L. 50. Sacrifice of Melchisedec. L.

Madrid. 287. Bridal Couple, 1523. 478. St. Jerome.

Milan. BRERA, 244. Pietà, 1545. 253. Portrait of Lady. 254. Portrait of Old Man. 255. Portrait of Man. All L.
GAL. OGGIONI, 16. Assumption of Virgin. E. 67. Portrait of Man.
POLDI-PEZZOLI, PINACOTECA, 86. Holy Family.
MUSEO CIVICO, 83. Portrait of Young Man.
BORROMEO, Christ on Cross with Symbols of the Passion.
DR. FRIZZONI, St. Catherine.

Monte S. Giusto (near Macerata). CHURCH, Crucifixion, 1531.

Munich. 1083. Marriage of St. Catherine. E.

Nancy. Head of a Man. L.

Naples. SALA VENETA, 56. Madonna with St. Peter Martyr. E. Bust of Man in white cap and coat (?). E.

Osimo. MUNICIPIO, Madonna and Angels.

Paris. 1349. Christ and Adulteress. 1350. St. Jerome, 1500. 1351. Nativity.

Ponteranica (near Bergamo). CHURCH, Altar-piece in six panels.

Recanati. MUNICIPIO, Altar-piece in six parts, 1508. Transfiguration. E.
S. DOMENICO, Fresco: S. Vincent in Glory.
S. MARIA SOPRA MERCANTI, Annunciation.
Rome. BORGHESE, 193. Madonna with S. Onofrio and a Bishop, 1508. 185. Portrait of Man.
CAPITOL, 176. Portrait of Man.
DORIA, 388. St. Jerome.
ROSPIGLIOSI, Allegory.
PRINCE DORIA, Portrait of Man.
Sedrina (near Bergamo). CHURCH, Madonna in Glory and four Saints, 1542.
St. Petersburg. LEUCHTENBERG COLLECTION, St. Catherine, 1521.
Trescorre. SUARDI CHAPEL, Frescoes, 1524.
Treviso. SALA SERNAGIOTTO, 20. Portrait of Monk, 1526.
S. CRISTINA, Altar-piece, Dead Christ (lunette). E.
Venice. CARMINE, S. Nicholas in Glory, 1529.
S. GIACOMO DALL' ORIO, Madonna and Saints, 1546.
S. GIOVANNI E PAOLO, S. Antonino bestowing Alms, 1542.
Vienna. 214. Santa Conversazione.
215. Portrait of Man.
220. Three Views of a Man.

BARTOLOMMEO MONTAGNA.

1450 circa–1523. Pupil of Alvise Vivarini; influenced by Gentile Bellini and the Paduan sculptor Bellano.

Belluno. 34. Madonna. E.
Bergamo. LOCHIS, 128. Madonna with SS. Roch and Sebastian, 1487.
MORELLI, 44. St. Jerome.
FRIZZONI-SALIS, Madonna.

Berlin.   44. Madonna, Saints, and Donors, 1500.
Bremen.   KUNSTHALLE, 16. Head and Hands of Madonna from an Annunciation.
Certosa (near Pavia). Madonna, SS. John, Onofrio, and three Angels.
London.   MR. C. BUTLER, Madonna.
             SIR WM. FARRER, Madonna. E. Two Cassone Tondi. L.
             MR. LUDWIG MOND, Madonna with St. Roch. E.
             SIR B. SAMUELSON, Madonna adoring Child.
Milan.   BRERA, 167. Madonna, four Saints, and three Angels, 1499.
             POLDI-PEZZOLI, St. Jerome. St. Paul. Two Tondi (on a cassone).
             DR. GUST. FRIZZONI, St. Jerome.
Modena.   5. Madonna, 1503.
Padua.   BISHOP'S PALACE, HALL, Frieze with Busts of Paduan Bishops.
             S. MARIA IN VANZO, Madonna and four Saints.
             SCUOLA DEL SANTO, Fresco 6. Opening of St. Anthony's Tomb.
Panshanger. LORD COWPER, Madonna.
Paris.   1393. Ecce Homo. 1394. Three Angels.
Praglia (near Padua). REFECTORY, fresco: Crucifixion.
Strassburg. 6. Holy Family.
Venice.   ACADEMY, 80. Madonna, SS. Sebastian and Jerome. 78. Christ between SS. Roch and Sebastian.
             LADY LAYARD, John the Baptist between two other Saints.
Verona.   76. Two Saints.
             S. NAZZARO E CELSO, SS. Nazzaro and Celso. SS. John and Benedict. Pietà. SS. Blaise and Giuliana. Frescoes: Legend of St. Blaise. All 1491-1493.

Vicenza. SALA V, 1. Holy Family. 2. Madonna enthroned, four Saints, three Angels. E. 3. Madonna with SS. Monica and Mary Magdalen. 5. Madonna. L. 6. Madonna. L. 8. Presentation in Temple. 9. S. Agnes. 17. Madonna with SS. John the Baptist and Onofrio. 19. Madonna. L.

DUOMO, Fresco: Nativity. Altar-piece, Madonna with SS. Catherine and Margaret. Frescoes: SS. Margaret and Catherine.

S. CORONA, Magdalen between four other Saints.
S. LORENZO, Fresco in Chapel L. of Choir.
MONTE BERICO, Pietà, 1500. Fresco: Pietà.

PALMA VECCHIO.

1480 circa–1528. Pupil of Giovanni Bellini; influenced by Giorgione.

Alnwick. DUKE OF NORTHUMBERLAND, Portrait of Lady, (landscape by Cariani.)
Bergamo. LOCHIS, 183. Madonna and two Saints. L.
Berlin. 197A. Head of Young Woman. E.
197B. Bust of Woman.
174. Portrait of Man.
Brunswick. Adam and Eve. E.
Buda-Pesth. 82. Madonna with St. Francis, (finished by Cariani.)
Cambridge. FITZ WILLIAM MUSEUM, Venus. L (in part).
Dresden. 188. Madonna with John the Baptist and St. Catherine.
189. Three Sisters.
190. Venus.
191. Holy Family with S. Catherine.
192 Meeting of Jacob and Rachel. L.
Florence. UFFIZI, 619. Judith. L.

THE VENETIAN PAINTERS. 119

Genoa. BRIGNOLE-SALE, Madonna with Magdalen and John. L.
Glasgow. 336. Holy Family, (finished by Cariani.)
Hamburg. CONSUL WEBER, Annunciation.
Hampton Court. 115. Santa Conversazione.
   240. Head of Woman. L.
London. 636. Portrait of Man.
   MR. BENSON, Santa Conversazione and Donor, (finished by Cariani.)
   MR. WICKHAM FLOWER, Santa Conversazione, (finished by Cariani.)
   MR. MOND, Bust of Woman. L.
Milan. BRERA, 290. SS. Helen, Constantine, Roch, and Sebastian. 172. Adoration of Magi, L., (finished by Cariani.)
Modena. MARCHESE LOTARIO RANGONI, Madonna and Saints.
Munich. 1108. Madonna, SS. Roch and Mary Magdalen.
Naples. SALA GRANDE, 28. Santa Conversazione, with male and female Donors.
Paris. 1399. Adoration of Shepherds and female Donor.
Peghera. CHURCH, Polyptych.
Rome. BORGHESE, 106. Lucrece. L. 163. Madonna, Francis, Jerome, and Donor.
   CAPITOL, 203. Christ and Adulteress.
   COLONNA, 22. Madonna, St. Peter, and Donor.
Serina. CHURCH, Polyptych.
Venice. ACADEMY, 310. Christ and Adulteress.
   302. St. Peter enthroned and six other Saints.
   315. Assumption of Virgin. L.
   QUIRINI-STAMPALIA, SALA IV, Unfinished Portrait of Young Woman. L.
   SALA XVII, Portrait of Man.
   GIOVANELLI, Sposalizio. L.
   S. MARIA FORMOSA, St. Barbara, Altar-piece.
   LADY LAYARD, Knight and Lady (a fragment).

Vicenza. S. STEFANO, Madonna and Saints.
Vienna. 134. John the Baptist.
139. The Visitation, (finished by Cariani.)
140. Santa Conversazione.
143. Portrait of Lady. L.
137. Violante. L.
133, 138, 141, 142, Busts of Women.
329^E. Portrait of Old Man.
136. Lucretia.
LICHTENSTEIN, Santa Conversazione. Holy Family and two female Saints. L.

SEBASTIANO DEL PIOMBO.

1485 circa–1547. Pupil of Giovanni Bellini, Cima, and Giorgione; later, influenced by Michelangelo.

Alnwick. DUKE OF NORTHUMBERLAND, Visitation.
Berlin. 237. Pietà. L. 259^A. Portrait of a Knight. L. 259^B. "Dorothea."
Broomhall, N. B. LORD ELGIN, Portrait of Roman Lady.
Buda-Pesth. Portrait of Raphael.
Cracow. PRINCE CZARTORYSKI, Portrait of (?) Raphael.
Florence. UFFIZI, 1123. "Fornarina," 1512. 592. Death of Adonis.
PITTI, 179. Martyrdom of St. Agatha, 1520. 409. Portrait of Man. L.
Linlathen, N. B. COL. ERSKINE, Portrait of Cardinal Nincofort. L.
London. 1. Resurrection of Lazarus, 1519. 24. Portrait of Lady. L. 1450. Holy Family and Donor.
Mr. BENSON, Portrait of Man. L.
DUKE OF GRAFTON, Carondelet and his Secretaries.
MR. LUDWIG MOND, Portrait of Pietro Aretino.

THE VENETIAN PAINTERS.   121

Naples.   SALA GRANDE, 56. Portrait of Ecclesiastic. L.
SALA VENETA, 15. Head of Clement VII. L.
SALA DEI CORREGGIO, 2. Holy Family. L.
Paris.   1352. Visitation, 1521. 1500. St. John in Desert.
M. ALPHONSE DE ROTHSCHILD, Violin Player.
Parma.   302. Clement VII. and a Chamberlain. L.
Rome.   PRINCE DORIA, Portrait of Andrea Doria. L.
SIG. DEL NERO, Portrait of a Prelate.
FARNESINA, SALA DI GALATEA, Frescoes in 8 lunettes, 1511.
S. MARIA DEL POPOLO, Birth of Virgin. L. (in part.)
S. PIETRO IN MONTORIO, Frescoes first Chapel Right.
St. Petersburg. Portrait of Cardinal Pole. L.
Siena.   PALAZZO SARACINI, Portrait of Man. L.
Treviso.   S. NICCOLÒ, Incredulity of Thomas. E.
Venice.   ACADEMY, 95. Visitation. (?) E.
LADY LAYARD, Pietà. E.
S. BARTOLOMMEO IN RIALTO, SS. Bartholomew, Louis, Sinibald, and Sebastian, on separate panels. E.
S. GIOVANNI CRISOSTOMO, St. John Chrysostom enthroned, and other Saints. E.
Vienna.   17. Portrait of (?) Cardinal Giulio di Medici.
Viterbo.   Pietà. L. 1525.

POLIDORO LANZIANI.

1515 (?) – 1565. Imitator of Titian ; influenced by Bonifazio and Pordenone ; later, by Paul Veronese.

Ashridge. LORD BROWNLOW, Christ and the Adulteress.
Badger Hall (Shropshire). MR. F. CAPEL-CURE, Madonna and kneeling Jerome. Madonna, St. Elizabeth, and Children.

Bergamo. MORELLI, 96. Holy Family.
Berlin. 159–160. Sporting Cupids.
173. Madonna and Saints.
NAZIONAL GALERIE, RACZYNSKI COLL., 6. St. Nicholas presenting children to the Virgin. L.
HERR WESENDONCK, 11. Portrait of Young Woman. 77. Madonna and Saints.
Boston, U. S. A. MRS. J. L. GARDNER, Portrait of Isabella D'Este.
Buda-Pesth. 96. Holy Family and St. Catherine.
113. Madonna and Young Bishop.
Cambridge. FITZWILLIAM MUSEUM, 145, 146. Sante Conversazioni.
Cologne. 730^K. Predelle: Nativity, Adoration, and Circumcision.
Dresden. 214. Madonna, Magdalen, and Venetian Noble.
215. Marriage of St. Catherine.
216. Madonna adoring Child.
219. Portrait of Man.
Edinburgh. 531. Holy Family.
Florence. PITTI, 52. Holy Family with St. Catherine and the Magdalen. 254. Holy Family, 269. Presentation in Temple. L.
Glasgow. 484. Holy Family with St. Dorothy.
Hampton Court. 173. Diana and Actæon.
Langton, N. B. (near Duns). MRS. BAILLIE-HAMILTON, Adoration of Magi.
Lille. 80. St. Peter Reading.
Linlathen, N. B. COL. ERSKINE, Madonna and St. Catherine.
London. LORD BATTERSEA, Madonna and infant John.
MR. R. BENSON, Madonna with St. Catherine and the Archangel Michael.
LORD BROWNLOW, Young Woman represented as Faith.
DORCHESTER HOUSE, Rest in Flight.

THE VENETIAN PAINTERS. 123

London (*Con.*). SIR WILLIAM FARRER, Three Ages. Holy Family and two Donors. Adoration of Shepherds.
MR. MOND, Madonna with St. Catherine and Holy Children.
MR. MUIR MACKENZIE, Madonna.
DUKE OF WESTMINSTER, Christ and the Adulteress.
LORD YARBOROUGH, Santa Conversazione. Christ at Emaus.

Modena. 115. Madonna and infant John.
Munich. 1109. Madonna, Bishop, and Donor.
1115. Portrait of Man with Staff (?).
Naples. SCUOLA VENETA, 2, 4. Allegories (tondi).
New Battle, N. B. MARQUIS OF LOTHIAN, Madonna with sleeping Child.
Oxford. CHRIST CHURCH, Diana and Actæon.
Paris. 669. Head of Young Woman.
1580. Holy Family.
1596. Holy Family and Saints.
Decapitation of Baptist.
MME. ANDRÉ, Morosini Family adoring Virgin. L.
Richmond. SIR FRANCIS COOK, Madonna and infant John.
Rome. BORGHESE, 91. Judith. 146. Madonna, Baptist, and an Angel.
CAPITOL, 20. Madonna and infant John.
DORIA, 127. Nativity. 418. Madonna with St. Catherine and the Baptist.
ROSPIGLIOSI, 10. Adoration of Shepherds.
DON MARCELLO MASSARENTI, Santa Conversazione.
Stuttgart. 34. Madonna with SS. Catherine and Jerome.
Venice. QUIRINI-STAMPALIA. SALA II, 144. Marriage of St. Catherine.
SALUTE, SACRISTY, Holy Family. Madonna.

Verona. 52. Madonna and infant John.
Vienna. 135. St. Roch.
         183. Adoration of Magi.
         384. Holy Family.
         394. Christ and the Magdalen.
         ACADEMY, 463. Finding of Moses.
         HARRACH COLLECTION, 305. Two Putti embracing.

G. A. PORDENONE.

1483-1540. Probably pupil of Alvise Vivarini. Developed under the influence of Giorgione and Titian.

Badger Hall (Shropshire). MR. F. CAPEL-CURE, Bust of Franciscan Cardinal.

Casarsa. OLD CHURCH, Frescoes: Story of True Cross, 1525.

Colalto (near Susigana). S. SALVATORE, Frescoes. E.

Cremona. DUOMO, Frescoes: Christ before Pilate; Way to Golgotha; Nailing to Cross; Crucifixion. All 1521. Altar-piece: Madonna enthroned with S. Dominic, Paul, and Donor, 1522. Fresco: Deposition, 1522.

Milan. DR. G. FRIZZONI, Dead Christ supported by Two Angels. E.

Motta di Livenza. S. MARIA DEI MIRACOLI, Frescoes: Annunciation.

Murano. S. MARIA DEGLI ANGELI, Annunciation. L.

Piacenza. MADONNA DI CAMPAGNA, Frescoes: Birth of Virgin; Adoration of Magi; Disputation of St. Catherine. Altar-piece; Marriage of St. Catherine. All 1529-1531.

Pordenone. DUOMO, Madonna covering with mantle six Donors, SS. Joseph and Christopher to R. and L., 1515. Fresco: SS. Erasmus and Roch, 1525. St. Mark enthroned, SS. Sebastian, Jerome, John, and Alexander, 1535.

THE VENETIAN PAINTERS. 125

Pordenone (*Con.*). MUNICIPIO, St. Gothard between SS. Roch and Sebastian, 1525.
San Daniele (near Udine). DUOMO, Trinity, 1535.
Spilimbergo. DUOMO, Assumption of Virgin. Conversion of St. Paul. Simon Magus, 1524.
Susigana. CHURCH, Madonna and four Saints. E.
Torre (near Pordenone). CHURCH, Madonna and four Saints.
Treviso. DUOMO, Adoration of Magi, and other frescoes, 1520.
Venice. ACADEMY, 305. Portrait of Lady. 298. Head of Man Praying. 323. Madonna of Carmel, Saints, and the Ottobon Family. 316. St. Lorenzo Giustiniani and three other Saints.
S. GIOVANNI ELEMOSINARIO, SS. Roch, Sebastian, and Catherine.
S. ROCCO, SS. Martin and Christopher, 1528.
S. STEFANO, Ruined Frescoes in Cloister.

ANDREA PREVITALI.

Active 1502-1525. Pupil of Giovanni Bellini; influenced by Lotto.
Bergamo. CARRARA, 25. Pentecost. 68. Marriage of St. Catherine. 97. Altar-piece in 8 parts. 182. Madonna, 1514. 183. Madonna, two Saints, and Portraits of Cassoti and his Wife. 184. Madonna.
LOCHIS, 171. Madonna. E. 176. Madonna with SS. Dominic and Sebastian, 1506.
SIG. BAGLIONI, Madonna and two Saints.
COUNT MORONI, Madonna, Saint, and Donor. Family Group.
S. ALESANDRO IN CROCE, Crucifixion, 1524.
S. ANDREA, Entombment.
DUOMO, Altar-piece, and three Predelle in Sacristry, 1524.

Bergamo (*Con.*). S. MARIA MAGGIORE, Fresco over S. Door.
S. SPIRITO, St. John the Baptist and four other Saints, 1515. Madonna between four female Saints, 1525.
Berlin. 39. Madonna and four Saints.
45. Marriage of St. Catherine.
Buda-Pesth. 77. Madonna.
Ceneda. S. MARIA DI MESCHIO, Annunciation. E.
Dresden. 60. Madonna and Saints, 1510.
Hamburg. CONSUL WEBER. 101. Holy Family.
Keir, N.B. MR. ARCH. STIRLING, Woman playing, and two Men.
London. 695. Madonna and Donor. E.
1173. Allegorical Subject.
SIR H. HOWARTH, Rest in Flight.
Milan. BRERA, 304. Christ in Garden, 1512. Coronation (lunette).
BONOMI-CEREDA, Madonna and two Saints, 1522.
DR. GUST. FRIZZONI, Madonna and Donor, 1506.
Oldenburg. 80. Baptist in Wilderness, 1521.
Oxford. CHRIST CHURCH LIBRARY, Madonna.
Padua. GAL. CAVALLI, 1423. Madonna and Donor, 1502.
Venice. PALAZZO DUCALE, CHAPEL, Christ in Limbo. Crossing of Red Sea.
LADY LAYARD, Head of Christ.
S. GIOBBE, Marriage of St. Catherine.
REDENTORE, Nativity. Crucifixion.
Verona. 151. Stoning of Stephen.
173. Immaculate Conception.
Vienna. 14. Madonna. E. 61. Portrait of Man.

ROCCO MARCONI.

Active in the earlier decades of the XVI century. Pupil of Giovanni Bellini and follower of Palma.

Berlin. 3. Christ Blessing (?). E.
196. Christ and the Adulteress.
Buda-Pesth. 100. Madonna, Saints, and Donor.
Chantilly. Madonna and Saints (ascribed to Palma).
Dresden. 64. Madonna and Saints.
Düsseldorf. 8. Triptych. E.
Leipzig. 255. Madonna and four Saints (?).
London. 1252. Death of Peter Martyr (?).
LORD ASHBURNHAM, Small Landscape (?).
MR. J. P. CARRINGTON, Bust of Man (?). E.
MR. C. BUTLER, Christ in Landscape Blessing.
LORD NORTHBROOK, Madonna. E.
SIR MICHAEL SHAW-STEWART, Madonna.
Munich. 1085. St. Nicholas of Bari, St. Andrew, and a Bishop.
Münster (in W.). 65. Madonna and Saints.
New Battle, N. B. MARQUIS OF LOTHIAN, Madonna.
Padua. 65. Madonna and Saints (?).
Richmond. SIR FRANCIS COOK, Madonna.
Christ and the Adulteress. Christ at Emaus.
Rome. CORSINI, 612. Christ Blessing.
Strassburg. 8. Madonna. E.
Stuttgart. 75. Last Supper. L.
Tours. 598. Madonna and Saints.
Venice. ACADEMY. 166. Deposition. 317. Christ between two Saints. 334. Christ and the Adulteress.
PALAZZO REALE, Christ and the Adulteress.
GIOVANELLI, Christ and the Adulteress.
S. CASSIANO, The Baptist and four Saints.
S. GIOVANNI E PAOLO, Christ and Saints.
Vienna. CZERNIN GALLERY, 30. Madonna.

N. RONDINELLI.

Active about 1480-1500. Pupil of Giovanni Bellini, whose name he often signs; slightly influenced by Palmezzano.

Berlin. 11. Madonna.
HERR WESENDONCK, 6. Madonna.
Fermo. CARMINE, Madonna and Saints.
Florence. UFFIZI, 354. Portrait of Man. 384. Madonna and two Saints.
Forli. 90. Madonna.
DUOMO, St. Sebastian.
SACRISTY, Visitation.
Frankfort a/M. 35. Madonna with St. Anne and the Baptist.
Innsbruck. 561. Dead Christ upheld by two Angels.
Liverpool. 33. Portrait of Man.
London. LADY ASHBURTON, Madonna.
DORCHESTER HOUSE, Bust of Boy.
SIR B. SAMUELSON, Madonna with SS. Catherine and Bartholomew.
Milan. BRERA, 176. Madonna, four Saints, and three Angels. 177. St. John appearing to Galla Placida.
MUSEO CIVICO, 97. Madonna, SS. Francis and Peter.
Oldenburg. 77. Madonna.
Padua. SALA EMO, Portrait of Young Man.
Paris. 1158. Madonna between SS. Peter and Sebastian.
Ravenna. 13. Madonna and four Saints. Madonna between SS. Catherine and John.
S. DOMENICO, four large pictures, probably Organ Shutters; Madonna, Gabriel, St. Peter Martyr, S. Dominic.
Rome. BARBERINI, 36, 54. Two Madonnas.
CAPITOL, Portrait of Man.
DORIA. 374. Madonna. E. 375. Madonna. 376. Madonna.

Rossie Priory, N. B. LORD KINNAIRD. Old Man and Young Man.
Stuttgart. 22. Madonna.
Venice. MUSEO CORRER, SALA VII, 19, Madonna.
SALA IX, 19. Madonna, two Saints, and two Donors.
GIOVANELLI, Two Madonnas.
LADY LAYARD, Madonna.
S. FANTINO, Holy Family.

GIROLAMO SAVOLDO.

Circa 1480-1548. Possibly pupil of Francesco Bonsignori; influenced by Bellini, Giorgione, Palma, and Lotto.

Berlin. 307. Mourning over Dead Christ.
307ᴬ. Magdalen.
Brescia. MARTINENGO, SALA C, Adoration of Shepherds.
Fermo. CASA BERNETTI, St. Jerome in Landscape. E.
Florence. UFFIZI, 645. Transfiguration.
MR. LOESER, St. Jerome.
Gosford House, N. B. LORD WEMYS, A Shepherd. Portrait of a Man holding a paper with both hands.
Hampton Court. 138. "Gaston de Foix." 139. Nativity and Donors, 1527.
London. 1031. Magdalen.
MR. DOETSCH, Bust of Man.
MR. MOND, Portrait of Man.
Milan. BRERA, 234. Madonna in Glory and four Saints.
AMBROSIANA, 52. Tranfiguration.
SIGNOR CRESPI, Bust of an Old Man.
Munich. LOTZBECK COLLECTION, 98. Rest in Flight.
New York, U. S. A. METROPOLITAN MUSEUM, MARQUAND COLLECTION, 272. Portrait of Man

Paris.	1518. "Gaston de Foix."
Rome.	VILLA BORGHESE, 139. Head of Youth.
	CAPITOL, 14. Portrait of Woman seated.
Seven Oaks.	LORD AMHERST, Flute-player,
Treviso.	SAN NICCOLÒ, Altar-piece, 1521.
Turin.	118. Nativity. 119. Adoration of Shepherds.
Urbino.	CASA ALBANI, Rest in Flight.
Venice.	328. The Hermits Antony and Paul.
	S. GIOBBE, Adoration of Shepherds.
	LADY LAYARD, St. Jerome.
Verona.	SANTA MARIA IN ORGANO, Madonna in Glory and Saints, 1533.
Vienna.	213. An Apostle. 208. Entombment.
	LICHTENSTEIN, 228. Portrait of Young Warrior. Dead Christ.

ANDREA MELDOLLA called SCHIAVONE.

1522 (?) – 1582. Pupil of Titian ; influenced by Parmigianino.

Amiens.	241. Calisto.
Badger Hall	(Shropshire). MR. F. CAPEL–CURE, Temperance.
Berlin.	170ᴬ. Parable of the Faithless Steward.
	170ᴮ. Parable of the Lord's Vineyard.
	182ᴬ. Mountain Landscape.
	182ᴮ. Forest Scene.
	HERR KAUFMANN, Madonna.
Buda-Pesth.	112. Head of Young Woman (?).
Chatsworth.	DUKE OF DEVONSHIRE, Preaching of Baptist. Marriage of Cupid and Psyche.
Dresden.	274. Pietà.
	275. Holy Family and Infant John.
Florence.	PITTI, 152. Death of Abel. 170. Adam and Eve.
	UFFIZI, 588. Adoration of Shepherds.

THE VENETIAN PAINTERS. 131

Gosford House, N. B. LORD WEMYS, Preparation for
        Combat. The Defence. Shepherd and Cattle.
        Infant Jupiter and Nymphs.
Hamburg. CONSUL WEBER, 107. Triumph.
Hampton Court. 88. Tobias and the Angel.
        175. Judgment of Midas.
        289. Christ before Pilate.
London.   LORD ASHBURNHAM, A Cassone.
        MR. R. BENSON, Landscape with Ruins.
        BRIDGEWATER HOUSE, Christ before Pilate.
           Last Supper. Marriage of St. Catherine.
        LORD BROWNLOW, St. Catherine.
        MR. C. BUTLER, Jason slaying Bulls of Aetos.
        SIR WILLIAM FARRER, St. Jerome.
        SIR H. HOWARTH, Dead Christ.
        MR. JAMES KNOWLES, Jupiter and Nymph.
Marseilles. Judith.
Milan.   MUSEO CIVICO, 124-126. Story of Esther.
Munich,   1089. Parnassus.
Naples.   SALA VENEZIANA, 53. Christ before Pilate.
Paris.   1524. The Baptist.
        1582. Ecce Homo.
Parma.   368. Deucalion and Pyrrha,
Venice.   ACADEMY, 271. Christ before Pilate. 324.
        Circumcision. 335. 337. Allegories.
        QUIRINI-STAMPALIA, SALA V, 89. Madonna and
           St. Catherine.
        CORRIDOR, Fancy Portrait of Lady.
           SALA XIV, 224. Conversion of St. Paul.
        PALAZZO REALE, Three ceiling paintings. Two
           Philosophers.
        S. M. DEL CARMINE, PARAPET OF ORGAN LOFT,
           Six pictures.
        S. GIACOMO DELL' ORIO. Christ at Emaus.
Vienna.   146. Christ before Caiphas.
        147. Portrait of Man.

Vienna (*Con.*). 148. Curius Dentatus.
    149. Madonna, infant John, and St. Catherine.
    158. Birth of Jupiter.
    159. Belshazzar's Feast.
    160. Jupiter nursed by Amalthea.
    168. Diana and Actæon.
    175. Queen of Sheba.
    184. David and the Ark.
    185. Cupid and Psyche.
    190. Scipio.
    194. Allegory of Music.
    195. Scene from Apocalypse.
    202. Apollo and Daphne.
    203. Death of Samson.
    204. Apollo and Cupid.
    261. Adoration of Shepherds.
    331. Mucius Scævola.

G. B. TIEPOLO.

1696–1770. Influenced by G. B. Piazzetta, formed on Paolo Veronese.

Amiens. 233, 234, 235, 236. Sketches.
Badger Hall (Shropshire). MR. F. CAPEL-CURE, Small Finding of Moses. Ceilings: Bride and Groom; Allegory.
Bergamo. CARRARA, 281, 282. Sketches.
    LOCHIS, 74. Sketch.
    SIGNOR BAGLIONI, Two legendary subjects.
    SIGNOR PICCINELLI, Christ in the Garden. Legendary subject.
    DUOMO, Martyrdom of St. John the Bishop.
    COLLEONI CHAPEL, Lunettes: Story of the Baptist.
Berlin. 454. After the Bath. 459. Reception. 459^A. St. Dominic and the Rosary. 459^B. Martyrdom of St. Agatha.

THE VENETIAN PAINTERS. 133

Brighton. MR. CONSTANTINE IONIDES, Apotheosis of a Pope.
Brussels. M. LÉON SOMZÉE, Sacrifice of Polyxena.
Buda-Pesth. 641. God the Father.
    649. Warrior Saint on horseback.
    651. Madonna and Saints.
Caen. 56. Sketch for Ecce Homo.
Edinburgh. 338. Finding of Moses.
    355. Antony and Cleopatra.
Frankfort a/M. 50. Court Scene.
Hamburg. CONSUL WEBER, 141. Christ bearing Cross.
    142. Crucifixion.
London.   1192, 1193. Sketches. 1333. Deposition.
   LORD BATTERSEA, Sketch of Madonna, Saints, and Angels.
   THE MISSES COHEN, Sketch of Esther and Ahasuerus.
   MRS. MARTIN COLNAGHI, Assumption.
   SIR W. M. CONWAY, Allegory of the Overthrow of Paganism.
   DR. RICHTER, Two Versions of Christ and Adulteress. Two legendary subjects.
Mayence. 124. An Encampment.
Milan. PALAZZO CHIERICI, Chariot of the Sun, ceiling fresco.
   NATURAL HISTORY MUSEUM, Frescoes.
   POLDI-PEZZOLI, PINACOTECA, 74. A Sketch.
   90. Madonna and Saints.
   SIGNOR CRESPI, St. Anne presenting Virgin to God, 1759.
Munich. 1271. Adoration of Magi. 1272, 1273. Historical subjects.
New York, U. S. A. METROPOLITAN MUSEUM, 18. Sacrifice of Isaac. 28. Triumph of Ferdinand III. Crowning with Thorns.
Padua. SALA ROMANINO, 654. St. Patrick.
   SANTO, Martyrdom of St. Agatha.

Paris. 1547. Christ at Emaus. 1549. Standard painted on both sides.
MME. ANDRÉ, Reception of Henry III (fresco). Three Ceiling frescoes.
M. LÉOPOLD GOLDSCHMIDT, Crucifixion.
Parma. 216. St. Antony Abbot.
Piove (near Padua). S. NICCOLÒ, Franciscan Saint in Ecstacy.
Richmond. SIR F. COOK. Esther and Ahasueras.
Rossie Priory, N. B. LORD KINNAIRD, Assumption.
Strassburg. St. Roch.
Turin. 293. St. Antony Abbot.
Udine. 31. Chapter of Maltese Order.
S. MARIA DELLA PIETÀ, Ceiling.
Venice. 484. S. Joseph, the Child, and four Saints.
462. Finding of True Cross.
PALAZZO DUCALE, SALA DI QUATTRO PORTE, Neptune and Venice.
SEMINARIO, REFECTORY, Christ at Emaus.
QUIRINI-STAMPALIA, SALA X, 219. Portrait of Procurator.
— PALAZZO LABIA, Frescoes: Antony and Cleopatra.
PALAZZO REZZONICO, Two Ceilings.
S. ALVISE, Christ at Column. Way to Golgotha.
S. APOSTOLI, Communion of S. Lucy.
S. FAVA, The Virgin and her Parents.
FRARI, Stations of the Cross.
— GESUATI, Ceiling. Altar-piece: Madonna and three female Saints.
S. GIOVANNI E PAOLO, Ceiling of R. Chapel.
S. MARIA DELLA PIETÀ, Ceiling.
— SCALZI, Ceiling.
SCUOLA DEL CARMINE, Ceiling paintings.
Verona. 70. Four Olivetan Saints.

Vicenza. ENTRANCE HALL, 1. Immaculate Conception.
VILLA VALMARANA, Frescoes in Villa and Casino, subjects from Homer, Virgil, Ariosto, and Tasso, also Costume Pieces, and Oriental Scenes.
Vienna. ACADEMY, 484. Sketch.
— Würzburg. ARCHBISHOP'S PALACE, Frescoes: Grand Staircase, 1753. Hall of Emperors, 1751.
CHAPEL, Two Altar-pieces.

JACOPO TINTORETTO.

1518-1592. May have been a pupil of Bonifazio Veronese; influenced by Titian, Parmigianino, and Michelangelo.

Augsburg. 265. Christ in the House of Martha.
Bergamo. CARRARA, 111. A Lady dressed as a Queen.
Berlin. 298. Portrait of Procurator.
299. The same.
300. Madonna with SS. Mark and Luke.
310. Luna, and the Hours.
316. Procurator before St. Mark.
HERR KAUFMANN, Bust of Old Man.
Bologna. 145. Visitation. CORRIDOR IV, Portrait of Man.
Boston, U. S. A. MRS. J. L. GARDNER, Portrait of Senator.
Brescia. TOSIO, SALA XIII, 14. An Old Man.
S. AFRA, Transgfiuration.
Buda-Pesth. 114. Head of Old Man.
Caen. 12. Deposition.
Cambridge, U. S. A. PROF. C. E. NORTON, Head of Old Man. Portrait of Senator of 83. L.
Carder House (near Glasgow). MR. ARCH. STIRLING, Portrait of Senator.
Cologne. 817. Ovid and Corinna.

Dresden.   174. Lady dressed in Mourning. 269. The Rescue. 270. Two Gentlemen.
Escurial.   Christ washing the feet of the Disciples.
Florence.   PITTI, 65, 70. Portraits of Men. 83. Portrait of Luigi Cornaro. 131. Portrait of Vincenzo Zeno.
            UFFIZI, 378. Portrait of himself. 577. Bust of Young Man. 601. Admiral Venier. 615. Portrait of Old Man. 638. Portrait of Jacopo Sansovino. 649. Portrait of Man.
Hamburg.   CONSUL WEBER, 117. Warrior.
Hampton Court. 69. Esther before Ahasuerus. 77. Nine Muses. 78. Portrait of Dominican. 91. Knight of Malta. 120. Portrait of a Senator.
Leipzig.   239. Resurrection.
Lille.   652. Portrait of a Senator.
London.   16. St. George and Dragon. 1130. Christ washing feet of Disciples. 1313. Origin of the Milky Way.
            BRIDGEWATER HOUSE. Portrait of Man.
            LORD BROWNLOW, Busts of two Old Men.
            MR. R. CRAWSHAY, Adam and Eve.
            MR. BUTLER, Moses striking Rock. Portrait of Senator.
            DORCHESTER HOUSE, Portrait of Man, 1548. Portrait of Man by Window.
            SIR WM. FARRER, The Resurrection.
            MR. ARTHUR JAMES, Portrait of Andrea Barbadigo. Portrait of Man.
            MR. MOND, Galleys at Sea. Portrait of Giovanni Gritti.
            LORD ROSEBERY, Portrait of Admiral Venier. E.
            MR. SALTING, Portrait of Ottavio di Strà, 1567.
Lübeck.   88. Raising of Lazarus, 1576.

Lucca.	SALA I, 45. Portrait of Man.
Lyons.	36. Danäe (in part).
Madrid.	410. Battle on Land and Sea.
	422. Joseph and Potiphar's Wife.
	423. Solomon and the Queen of Sheba.
	424. Susanna and the Elders.
	425. Finding of Moses.
	426. Esther before Ahasuerus.
	427. Judith and Holofernes
Milan.	BRERA, 217. Pietá. 230. St. Helen, three other Saints, and two Donors. 234 bis. Finding of Body of St. Mark. E.
	MUSEO CIVICO, 86. Bust of Procurator.
Newport, U. S. A.	MR. T. H. DAVIS, Bust of Man.
Panshanger.	LORD COWPER, Portrait of Man.
Paris.	1464. Susanna and the Elders. 1465. Paradise. 1467. Portrait of Old Man.
Richmond.	SIR F. COOK, St. John the Baptist. Portrait of Senator.
Rome.	CAPITOL, 248. The Baptism. 249. Ecce Homo. 250. The Flagellation.
	COLONNA, 4. Three Women and a Man adoring the Holy Spirit. 113. Old Man playing Spinnet. 94, 95. Portraits of Men.
	DORIA, 265. Portrait of Man. E.
Turin.	162. The Trinity.
Venice.	ACADEMY, 225. S. Giustina and three Donors, 1580.
	210. Madonna, three Saints, and three Donors, 1566.
	242. Portrait of Carlo Morosini.
	Portrait of a Senator.
	217. Deposition.
	241. Senator in Prayer.
	245. Portrait of Jacopo Soranzo, 1564.
	234. Andrea Capello. E.

Venice (*Con.*). SALA IV, Ceiling : Prodigal Son, Four Virtues.
    41. Death of Abel.
    244. Two Senators.
    42. Miracle of St. Mark, 1548.
    43. Adam and Eve.
    240. Two Senators.
    227. Resurrected Christ blessing three Senators.
    239. Madonna, and three portraits.
    213. Crucifixion.
    215. Resurrection.
PALAZZO DUCALE, COLLEGIO, Doge Mocenigo recommended to Christ by St. Mark. Figures in *grisaille* around the Clock.
Doge Daponte before the Virgin.
Marriage of St. Catherine and Doge Donà.
Doge Gritti before the Virgin.
ANTI-COLLEGIO, Mercury and three Graces. Vulcan's Forge. Bacchus and Ariadne. Minerva expelling Mars: All, 1578.
ANTE-ROOM OF CHAPEL, SS. Margaret, George, and Louis.
SS. Andrew and Jerome
SENATO, St. Mark presenting Doge Loredan to the Virgin in presence of two other Saints.
SALA QUATTRO PORTE, Ceiling (in part).
INGRESSO, Lorenzo Amelio, 1570. Alessandro Bono. Vincenzo Morosini, 1580. Nicolo Priuli. Ceiling.
PASSAGE TO COUNCIL OF TEN, Andrea Delphino, 1573. A. Cicogna.
Federigo Contarini, 1570.
Nobles Illumined by the Holy Spirit.
SALA DEL GRAN CONSIGLIO, Paradise, 1590.
SALA DELLO SCRUTINO, Battle of Zara.

Venice (*Con.*). PALAZZO REALE LIBRERIA, Transportation of
    Body of St. Mark.
    St. Mark rescues a shipwrecked Saracen.
    Diogenes, Archimedes, and two other philo-
        sophers on separate canvases : All E.
    ANOTHER ROOM, St. Roch.
    PRINCE GIOVANELLI, Battle Piece. Portrait of
        Senator. Portrait of General. Portrait of
        Warrior.
    S. CASSIANO, Crucifixion. Christ in Limbo.
        Resurrection.
    GESUITI, Assumption of Virgin. Circumcision.
    S. GIORGIO MAGGIORE, Last Supper. Gather-
        ing of Manna. Entombment.
    S. GIUSEPPE DI CASTELLO, Michael overcoming
        Lucifer.
    S. MARIA MATER DOMINI, Finding of True
        Cross.
    S. MARIA DELL' ORTO, Last Judgment. E.
        Martyrdom of Paul. The Tablets of the
        Law and the Golden Calf. E. Martyrdom
        of St. Agnes. Presentation of Virgin. E.
    S. MARZIALE, Glory of S. Marziale.
    S. PAOLO, Last Supper. Assumption of Virgin.
    S. ROCCO, Annunciation. Pool of Bethesda.
        St. Roch and the Beasts of the Field. St.
        Roch healing the Sick. St. Roch in Campo
        d'Armata. St. Roch consoled by an Angel.
        St. Roch before the Pope.
    SCUOLA DI S. ROCCO, Ground Floor, nearly
        all the paintings on walls.
    STAIRCASE, Visitation.
    UPPER FLOOR, Hall, All the paintings on
        walls and ceiling. Portrait of himself, 1573.
    INNER ROOM, Crucifixion, 1565. Christ before
        Pilate. Ecce Homo. Way to Golgotha.

Venice (*Con.*). Ceiling, 1560. Altogether, sixty-two paintings.
   SALUTE, Marriage of Cana, 1561.
   S. SILVESTRO, Baptism.
   S. STEFANO. Last Supper. Washing of Feet. Agony in Garden.
   S. TROVASO, Temptation of St. Anthony.
   S. ZACCARIA, Birth of Virgin.
Vicenza. ENTRANCE HALL. 42. St. Augustine healing the Plague-stricken.
Vienna. 417. St. Jerome. E.
   239. Susanna and the Elders. E.
   236. Sebastian Venier.
   244. An Officer in Armour.
   235. Old Man and Boy.
   242, 245. Portraits of Men.
   250. Portrait of Man, 1553.
   482. Portrait of Old Man.
   255, 258, 486. Portraits of Men.
   249. Portrait of Lady.
   ACADEMY, 13. Portrait of Ales. Contarini. 34. Portrait of Doge Priuli.
Woburn Abbey. 36. Portrait of Man. L.

TITIAN.

1477–1576. Pupil of the Bellini; formed by Giorgione.
Ancona. 8. Crucifixion. L.
   S. DOMENICO, Madonna with SS. Francis, Blaise, and Donor, 1520.
Antwerp. 357. Alexander VI presenting Baffo to St. Peter. E.
Ascoli. St. Francis receiving the Stigmata. L.
Berlin. 160A. Infant Daughter of Roberto Strozzi, 1542.

Berlin (*Con.*). 163. Portrait of himself. L.
            166. His own Daughter Lavinia.
Boston.   MRS. J. L. GARDNER, Rape of Europa, 1562.
Brescia.   S. NAZARO E CELSO, Altar-piece, 1522.
Cobham Hall. LORD DARNLEY, Portrait of Ariosto. E.
Dresden. 168. Madonna with four Saints. E.
           169. Tribute Money. E.
           170. Lavinia as Bride, 1555.
           171. Lavinia as Matron. L.
           172. Portrait of Man, 1561.
           173. A Lady with a Vase. L.
           175. Madonna with a Family as Donors (in part only). L.
           176. Lady in Red Dress.
Florence. PITTI, 18. "La Bella," Eleanora Gonzaga, Duchess of Urbino.
           54. Pietro Aretino, 1545.
           67. Magdalen.
           92. Portrait of Young Man.
           185. The Concert. E.
           200. Philip II.
           201. Ippolito de' Medici, 1533.
           215. Full-length Portrait of Man.
           228. Head of Christ.
           495. "Tommaso Mosti."
        UFFIZI, 599. Eleanora Gonzaga, Duchess of Urbino, 1537.
           605. Fr. Maria della Rovere, Duke of Urbino, 1537.
           626. Flora. E.
           633. Madonna with St. Antony Abbot. E.
           1108. Venus—the head a portrait of Lavinia. L.
           1116. Portrait of Beccadelli, 1552.
           1117. Venus—the head a portrait of Eleanora Gonzaga.

WORKS OF

Genoa. BALBI-SENAREGA, Madonna with SS. Catherine, Domenic, and a Donor. E.

Hampton Court. 113. Portrait of Man, 1546. 149. Portrait of Man. E.

London. 4. Holy Family and Shepherd.
35. Bacchus and Ariadne. 1523.
270. "Noli me Tangere." E.
635. Madonna with SS. John and Catherine, 1533.
BRIDGEWATER HOUSE, Holy Family. E.
"The Three Ages." E.
Venus rising from the Sea.
Diana and Actæon. 1559.
Calisto. 1559.
MR. MOND, Madonna. L.

Madrid. 236. Madonna with SS. Ulfus and Bridget. E.
450. Bacchanal.
451. Venus Worship.
452. Alfonso of Ferrara, 1518.
453. Charles V and his dog, 1533.
454. Philip II in Armour, 1550.
456. The Forbidden Fruit. L.
457. Charles V on Horseback, 1548.
458. Danaë, 1554.
459. Venus, and Youth playing Organ. L.
461. Salome (Portrait of Lavinia).
462. Trinity, 1554.
463. Knight of Malta. L.
464. Entombment, 1559.
465. Sisyphus. L.
466. Prometheus. L.
469. St. Margaret. L.
470. Philip II offering Infant Don Fernando to Victory. L.
471. Allocution of Alfonso d'Avalos, 1541.
476. Religion succoured by Spain. L.

THE VENETIAN PAINTERS. 143

Madrid (*Con.*). 477. Portrait of himself.
    480. Portrait of Man.
    485. The Empress Isabel, 1544.
Maniago.   CASA MANIAGO, Portraits of Irene and of Emilia di Spilimbergo. L.
Medole (near Brescia). DUOMO, Christ appearing to his Mother. L.
Milan.   BRERA, 248. St. Jerome. L.
    288. bis. Antonio Porcia.
Munich.   1110. "Vanitas." E.
    1111. Portrait of Man. E.
    1112. Portrait of Charles V, 1548.
    1113. Madonna. L.
    1114. Christ crowned with Thorns. L.
Naples.   SCUOLA VENETA, 11. Philip II. 20. Paul III, Ottaviano, and Card. Farnese, 1545.
Padua.   SCUOLA DEL SANTO, Frescoes : St. Anthony granting Speech to an Infant. The Youth who cut off his own leg. The Jealous Husband. All, 1511.
Paris.   1577. Madonna with SS. Stephen, Ambrose, and Maurice. E.
    1578. "La Vierge au Lapin."
    1579. Madonna with St. Agnes.
    1581. Christ at Emaus. L.
    1583. Crowning with Thorns. L.
    1584. Entombment.
    1585. St. Jerome. L.
    1587. "Venus del Prado." L.
    1588. Portrait of Francis I.
    1589. Allegory.
    1590. " Alfonso of Ferrara and Laura Dianti.
    1591. Portrait of Man with Hand in Belt.
    1592. "The Man with the Glove." E.
    1593. Portrait of Man with Black Beard.
Rome.   BORGHESE. 147. Sacred and Profane Love. E.

Rome (*Con.*). 188. St. Dominic. L. 170. Education of Cupid. L.
    CAPITOL, 145. Baptism, with Zuane Ram as Donor. E.
    DORIA, Daughter of Herodias. E.
    VATICAN, Madonna in Glory with six Saints, 1523.
    PRINCE CHIGI, Portrait of Aretino.

Serravalle. DUOMO, Madonna in Glory, with SS. Peter and Andrew, 1547.

Treviso. DUOMO, Annunciation.

Urbino. 39. The Resurrection. L.
    42. Last Supper. L.

Venice. ACADEMY, 426. Presentation of Virgin in Temple, 1540. 314. St. John in the Desert. 40. Assunta, 1518. 400. Pietà, begun in 1573, not quite finished at Titian's death.
    PALAZZO DUCALE, Staircase to Doge's private apartments, Fresco: St. Christopher, 1523.
    SALA DI QUATTRO PORTE, Doge Grimani before Faith, 1555.
    PALAZZO REALE, on ceiling of ante-room to Libreria, Wisdom. L.
    GIOVANELLI, Portrait of Man. L.
    FRARI, Pesaro Madonna, 1526.
    GESUITI, Martyrdom of St. Lawrence. L.
    S. GIOVANNI ELEMOSINARIO, St. John the Almsgiver, 1533.
    S. LIO, St. James of Compostella. L.
    S. MARCUOLO, The Christ Child between SS. Catherine and Andrew. E.
    S. MARZIALE, Tobias and the Angel, 1540.
    SCUOLA DI S. ROCCO, Annunciation. Dead Christ (?). E.
    SALUTE, Descent of Holy Spirit. L.
    Ceiling of CHOIR: Eight Medallions, one a

Venice (*Con.*). Portrait of Titian himself, the rest Heads of Saints.
 SACRISTY, St. Mark between SS. Roch, Sebastian, Cosmos, and Damian. E.
 Ceiling, David and Goliath.
 Sacrifice of Isaac. Cain slaying Abel.
 S. SALVATORE, Annunciation. L. Transfiguration, L.
 S. SEBASTIANO, St. Nicholas of Bari (in part), 1563.

Verona. 51. Portrait of Ferdinand, King of the Romans.
 DUOMO, Assumption of Virgin.

Vienna. 176. "Gipsy Madonna." E.
 180. "Madonna with the Cherries." E.
 178. "The Large Ecce Homo," 1543.
 181. "The Little Tambourine Player." E.
 163. Isabella d'Este, 1534.
 197. "Das Mädchen im Pelz" (Eleanora Gonzaga).
 177. "Benedetto Varchi."
 167. "The Physician Parma." E.
 191. John Frederick of Saxony, 1548.
 182. Jacopo di Strada, 1566.
 186. Shepherd and Nymph. L.
 CZERNIN, Portrait of Doge Gritti.

GIROLAMO DA TREVISO, THE YOUNGER.

1497-1544. Pupil of his father, P. M. Pennachi; influenced by Catena, Giorgione, and later by Dosso Dossi and Raphael.

Bologna. S. GIOVANNI IN MONTE, 1ST ALTAR R. Noli me Tangere. E.
 S. PETRONIO, 9TH CHAPEL R. Monochrome frescoes: Miracles of St. Antony of Padua.

WORKS OF

Dresden.   99. Adoration of Magi.
Faenza.   LA MAGIONE, CHOIR, Frescoes : Madonna and Saints, with Sabba Castiglione as Donor, 1533.
Ferrara.   SIG. SANTINI, A female Saint and five Men.
London.   263. Madonna, Saints, and Donor.
           MR. MOND, Bust of Young Man.
           DUKE OF WESTMINSTER, Nativity. St. Luke painting the Virgin.
Milan.   SIG. BAGATI-VALSECCHI, The Forge of Vulcan (fresco on chimney-piece).
Modena.   S. PIETRO, Holy Family with infant John and St. Catherine.
Münster (in W.). KUNSTVEREIN, 64. The Saviour (?).
Rome.   COLONNA, 109. Portrait of Man.
           DONNA LAURA MINGHETTI, Judgment of Paris (?).
Trent.   CASTLE, CHAPEL, Frescoes.
           INNER ROOM, Frieze.
           NOS. 4 AND 6 PIAZZA GRANDE, AND 12 VIA DEL TEATRO, Frescoes on façades.
Venice.   SALUTE, SACRISTY, St. Roch between SS. Sebastian and Jerome. E.
Verona.   121. Annunciation (?).
Vienna.   E. 512. Portrait of Man.

PAOLO VERONESE.

1528–1588. Pupil of Antonio Badile ; strongly influenced by Dom. Brusasorci.

Dresden.   224. Madonna with Cuccina Family.
           225. Adoration of Magi.
           226. Marriage of Cana.
           229. Finding of Moses (in part only).
           236. Portrait of Daniel Barbaro.

Florence.   PITTI, 216. Portrait of Daniel Barbaro.
            UFFIZI, 589. Martyrdom of S. Giustina. E.
            1136. Holy Family and St. Catherine.
Hampton Court. Madonna and Saints (?).
London.   26. Consecration of St. Nicholas.
            294. Alexander and the Family of Darius.
            DR. RICHTER, Holy Family. E.
Madrid.   528. Christ and the Centurion.
            532. Finding of Moses (?).
Maser.   VILLA BARBARO, Frescoes.
Milan.   BRERA, 227. SS. Antony, Cornelius, and Cyprian, and Page.
Padua.   S. GIUSTINA, Martyrdom of St. Giustina.
Paris.   1196. Christ at Emaus.
            1199. Young Mother and Child. E.
            1192. Marriage of Cana.
Rome.   COLONNA, 90. Portrait of Man in Green.
            VILLA BORGHESE, 101. St. Antony preaching to the Fishes.
Venice.   ACADEMY, 212. Battle of Lepanto. 203. Feast in House of Levi, 1573. 37. Madonna with SS. Joseph, John, Francis, Jerome, and Giustina.
            PALAZZO DUCALE, COLLEGIO, Thanksgiving for Lepanto.
            ANTE-COLLEGIO, Rape of Europa.
            S. BARNABÀ, Holy Family.
            S. CATERINA, Marriage of St. Catherine.
            S. FRANCESCO DELLA VIGNA, Holy Family with SS. Catherine and Antony Abbot.
            S. SEBASTIANO, Madonna and two Saints. Crucifixion. Madonna in Glory with St. Sebastian and other Saints. SS. Mark and Marcilian led to Martyrdom (in part). St. Sebastian being Bound (?).
            Frescoes: SS. Onofrio and Paul the Hermit.

Venice (*Con.*). SS. Matthew and Mark. SS. Roch, Andrew, Peter, and Figure of Faith. Tiburtine and Cumæan Sibyls.
Verona. 267. Portrait of Pasio Guadienti, 1556.
245. Deposition (?).
S. GIORGIO, Martyrdom of St. George.
S. PAOLO, Madonna and Saints. E.
Vicenza. SALA II, 12. Madonna.
MONTE BERICO, Feast of St. Gregory, 1572.
Vienna. 396. Christ at the House of Jairus.

ALVISE VIVARINI.

Active 1461-1503. Pupil of his uncle Bartolommeo.

Berlin. 38. Madonna enthroned with six Saints.
1165. Madonna enthroned with four Saints. L.
Florence. MR. CHARLES LOESER, Madonna.
Gosford House, N. B. LORD WEMYS, Bust of Smooth-faced Man.
London. THE MISSES COHEN, Bust of a Venetian Noble.
MR. SALTING, Portrait of Youth.
Milan. BRERA, Dead Christ adored by two Angels. E.
BONOMI-CEREDA, Portrait of Man, 1497.
SIGNOR BAGATI-VALSECCHI, S. Giustina dei Borromei. L.
Modena. 319. Portrait of Man (?).
Montefiorentino. Polyptych, 1475.
Naples. SCUOLA VENETA, 1. Madonna with SS. Francis and Bernardino, 1485.
Padua. 1371. Portrait of a Man.
Paris. 1519. Portrait of a Man. L.
COUNTESS DE BÉARN, Portrait of Man. L.
Venice. ACADEMY, 619. St. Matthew. 618. St. John the Baptist. 621. St. Sebastian. St. Antony Abbot. St. John Baptist. St. Laurence. E. 593. St. Clare. 87. Head of

Venice (*Con.*). Christ. L. 607. Madonna and six Saints, 1480.
          Museo Correr, Sala IX, 44. St. Antony of Padua.
          Frari, St. Ambrose enthroned and Saints. Begun in 1503, finished by Basaiti.
          S. Giovanni in Bragora, Madonna: Head of Christ, 1493 : Resurrection, 1498 : Predelle to last. Busts of Saviour, John, and Mark.
          S. Giovanni e Paolo, Christ bearing Cross.
          Redentore, Sacristy, Madonna.
          Lady Layard, Portrait of Man.
          Seminario, Stanza del Patriarca, Portrait of Man. L.
Vienna. 12. Madonna, 1489.
          Academy, St. Clare. Female Saint with Monstrance.
Windsor Castle. Portrait of Man with Hawk.

BARTOLOMMEO VIVARINI.

Active 1450–1499. Pupil of Giovanni and Antonio da Murano; influenced by Paduans.

Bergamo. Frizzoni-Salis, Madonna and two Saints.
Boston, U. S. A. Mr. Quincy Shaw, Magdalen.
Fermo. Count Bernetti, SS. Francis and James.
Gosford House, N. B. Lord Wemys, Polyptych. E.
London. 284. Madonna with SS. Paul and Jerome.
Meiningen. Ducal Palace, An Apostle.
Naples. Sala Veneta, 5. Madonna enthroned, 1465.
Paris. 1607. St. John Capistrano, 1459.
Turin. 780. Madonna, 1481.
Venice. Academy, 615, 1. Altar-piece in five parts, 1464. 584. Mary Magdalen. 585. St. Barbara, 1490.
          Frari, Madonna and four Saints, 1482.

150 WORKS OF THE VENETIAN PAINTERS.

Venice (*Con.*). S. GIOVANNI IN BRAGORA, Madonna between SS. Andrew and John, 1478.
S. GIOVANNI E PAOLO, St. Augustine, 1473. SS. Dominic and Lawrence.
S. MARIA FORMOSA, Triptych : Madonna, Birth of Virgin, Meeting of Joachim and Anne, 1473.

Vienna. 10. St. Ambrose between SS. Peter, Louis, Paul, and Sebastian, 1477.

INDEX OF PLACES.

Albi. Guardi.
Alnwick. DUKE OF NORTHUMBERLAND : Licinio, Palma.
S. del Piombo.
Alzano. CHURCH : Lotto.
Amiens. Guardi, Schiavone, Tiepolo.
Ancona. GALLERY : Crivelli, Lotto, Titian.
S. DOMENICO : Titian.
Antwerp. GALLERY : Antonello, Titian.
Ascoli. DUOMO : Crivelli.
GALLERY : Titian.
Ashridge. LORD BROWNLOW : Bassano, Bordone, Cariani, Polidoro.
Asolo. CHURCH : Lotto.
Augsburg. GALLERY : Barbari, Bassano, Tintoretto.
Badger Hall (Shropshire). MR. F. CAPEL-CURE : Basaiti, Guardi, Pordenone, Schiavone, Tiepolo.
Balcarres, N. B. LORD CRAWFORD : Licinio.
Basel. Cariani.
Bassano. GALLERY : Bassano, Guardi.
DUOMO, and S. GIOVANNI : Jacopo Bassano.
S. M. DELLE GRAZIE : J. Bassano.
Belluno. Bartolommeo Veneto, Beccaruzzi, Montagna.
Bergamo. GALLERY, CARRARA COLLECTION : Bartolommeo Veneto, Basaiti, Bassano, Bonifazio, Cariani, Gatena, Lotto, Previtali, Tintoretto.

Bergamo (*Con*.). LOCHIS COLLECTION: Antonello, Barbari, Bartolommeo Veneto, Basaiti, Beccaruzzi, Giovanni Bellini, Bonsignori, Bordone, Cariani, Crivelli, Guardi, Licinio, Lotto, Montagna, Palma Vecchio, Previtali.

MORELLI COLLECTION: Basaiti, Giovanni Bellini, Cariani, Cima, P. Longhi, Montagna, Polidoro.

SIGNOR BAGLIONI: Bassano, Cariani, Guardi, Longhi, Previtali, Tiepolo.

FRIZZONI-SALIS: Barbari, Basaiti, Bassano, Bonifazio, Montagna, Bartolommeo Vivarini.

CONTE MORONI: Guardi, Previtali.

SIGNOR PICCINELLI: Cariani, Licinio, Lotto, Tiepolo.

CONTE RONCALLI: Cariani.

CONTE SUARDI: Cariani, Bassano.

S. ALESSANDRO in COLONNA: Lotto.

S. ALESSANDRO IN CROCE: Lotto.

S. ANDREA: Previtali.

S. BARTOLOMMEO: Lotto.

S. BERNARDINO: Lotto.

COLLEONI CHAPEL: Tiepolo.

DUOMO: Cariani, Previtali, Tiepolo.

S. MARIA MAGGIORE: Lotto, Previtali.

S. MICHELE: Lotto.

S. SPIRITO: Lotto, Previtali.

Berlin. Antonello, Barbari, Basaiti, Giovanni Bellini, Bissolo, Bordone, Caprioli, Cariani, Carpaccio, Catena, Cima, Crivelli, Giorgione, Guardi, Lotto, Montagna, Palma, Sebastiano del Piombo, Polidoro, Previtali, Rocco Marconi, Rondinelli, Savoldo, Schiavone, Tiepolo, Tintoretto, Titian, Alvise Vivarini, Bartolommeo Vivarini.

INDEX OF PLACES. 153

Berlin (*Con.*). NAZIONAL GALERIE, RACYNSKI COLLECTION :
　　　　　Catena, Polidoro.
　　　　　HERR BECKERATH : Basaiti.
　　　　　HERR KAUFMANN : Basaiti, Bassano, Beccaruzzi, Schiavone, Tintoretto.
　　　　　HERR WESENDONCK : Bassano, Beccaruzzi, Polidoro, Rondinelli.
Biel, N. B. MRS. HAMILTON OGILVIE : Bassano, Canale, Guardi.
Bologna. GALLERY : Bassano, Cima, Tintoretto.
　　　　　S. GIOVANNI IN MONTE : Girolamo da Treviso.
　　　　　S. PETRONIO : Girolamo da Treviso.
Boston, U. S. A. MUSEUM : Basaiti, Beccaruzzi.
　　　　　MRS. J. L. GARDNER: Bonifazio, Catena, Guardi, Polidoro, Tintoretto, Titian.
　　　　　MR. J. QUINCY SHAW : Cima, Licinio, Bartolommeo Vivarini.
Bremen. KUNSTHALLE : Montagna.
Brescia. GALLERY TOSIO : Bissolo, Lotto, Tintoretto.
　　　　　S. AFRA : Tintoretto.
　　　　　S. ALESSANDRO : Jacopo Bellini.
　　　　　S. NAZARO E CELSO : Titian.
Brighton. MR. CONSTANTINE IONIDES : Guardi, Tiepolo.
　　　　　MR. HENRY WILLETT : Caprioli, Licinio.
Broomhall, N. B. LORD ELGIN : S. del Piombo
Brunswick. GALLERY : Palma Vecchio.
Brussels. Bassano, Crivelli, Guardi.
　　　　　M. LÉON SOMZÉE : Bart. Veneto, Tiepolo.
Buda-Pesth. Basaiti, Bassano, Beccaruzzi, Gentile Bellini, Cariani, Catena, Crivelli, Giorgione, Guardi. Licinio, Palma, S. del Piombo, Polidoro, Previtali, Rocco Marconi, Schiavone, Tiepolo, Tintoretto.
　　　　　HERR RATH : Licinio.
Caen. Carpaccio, Tiepolo, Tintoretto.
Cambridge. FITZWILLIAM MUSEUM : Beccaruzzi, Guardi, Palma, Polidoro.

INDEX OF PLACES.

Cambridge, U. S. A. PROF. C. E. NORTON: Licinio, Longhi, Tintoretto.
Campo S. Piero. ORATORY OF S. ANTONIO: Bonifazio (in part).
Carder House (near Glasgow). MR. ARCHIBALD STIRLING: Tintoretto.
Casarsa. PARISH CHURCH: Pordenone.
Castelfranco. CHURCH: Giorgione.
Castle Barnard. BOWES MUSEUM: Caprioli.
Celana (near Bergamo). Lotto.
Ceneda. MADONNA DI MESCHIO: Previtali.
Certosa (near Pavia). Montagna.
Chantilly. DUC D' AUMALE: Bissolo, Rocco Marconi.
Chatsworth. DUKE OF DEVONSHIRE: Bassano, Bordone, Cariani, Schiavone.
Cingoli. S. DOMENICO: Lotto.
Cittadella. DUOMO: Bassano.
Cobham Hall. LORD DARNLEY: Titian.
Colalto. S. SALVATORE: Pordenone.
Cologne. GALLERY: Bordone, Catena, Polidoro, Tintoretto.
Conegliano. DUOMO: Beccaruzzi, Cima.
S. M. DELLE GRAZIE: Beccaruzzi.
S. ROCCO: Beccaruzzi.
Costa di Mezzate (near Gorlago). Lotto.
Cracow. PRINCE CZARTORYSKI: S. del Piombo.
Cremona. DUOMO: Pordenone.
Dijon. Bassano, Caprioli.
Douai. Bartolommeo Veneto.
Dresden. Antonello, Barbari, Bartolommeo Veneto, Bassano, Beccaruzzi, Bonifazio, Bordone, Canaletto, Catena, Cima, Giorgione, Licinio, Longhi, Lotto, Palma Vecchio, Polidoro, Previtali, Rocco Marconi, Tintoretto, Titian, Girolamo da Treviso, Veronese.
Düsseldorf. Bissolo, Cima, Rocco Marconi.

INDEX OF PLACES. 155

Edinburgh. Bassano, Bordone, Guardi, Polidoro, Tiepolo.
Escurial. Tintoretto.
Faenza. LA MAGIONE: Gir. da Treviso
Feltre. SEMINARIO: Bassano.
Fermo. CARMINE: Rondinelli.
CASA BERNETTI: Savoldo, B. Vivarini.
Ferrara. Beccaruzzi, Carpaccio.
SIG. VENDEGHINI: Jacopo Bellini.
SIG. SANTINI: Girolamo da Treviso.
Florence. PITTI: Barbari, Bonifazio, Bordone, S. del Piombo, Polidoro, Schiavone, Tintoretto, Titian, Veronese.
UFFIZI: Bartolommeo Veneto, Bassano, Beccaruzzi, Giovanni Bellini, Bordone, Canaletto, Carpaccio, Giorgione, Licinio, Lotto, Palma Vecchio, S. del Piombo, Rondinelli, Schiavone, Tintoretto, Titian, Veronese.
PALAZZO PANCIATICHI: Crivelli.
MR. LOESER: Savoldo, Longhi, Alvise Vivarini.
Fonthill (Wilts). MR. ALFRED MORRISON, Bonsignori.
Forli. GALLERY: Rondinelli.
DUOMO: Rondinelli.
S. MERCURIALE, Rondinelli.
Frankfort (a/M.) GALLERY: Bartolommeo Veneto, Gentile Bellini, Canale, Carpaccio, Cima, Crivelli, Tiepolo.
Genoa. BRIGNOLE-SALE: Bordone, Licinio, Palma Vecchio.
PRINCE GIORGIO DORIA: Bartolommeo Veneto.
PALAZZO BALBI-SENAREGA: Titian.
S. ANNUNZIATA: Bissolo.
Glasgow. Bart. Veneto, Beccaruzzi, Bordone, Cariani, Catena, Guardi, Palma, Polidoro.
Gosford House, N. B. LORD WEMYS: Bassano, Bonsignori, Bordone, Savoldo, Schiavone, Alvise and Bart. Vivarini.

INDEX OF PLACES.

Hague. GALLERY: Bonifazio.
Haigh Hall (near Wigan). LORD CRAWFORD: Beccaruzzi, Carpaccio.
Hamburg. CONSUL WEBER: Barbari, Guardi, Lotto, Palma, Previtali, Schiavone, Tiepolo, Tintoretto.
Hampton Court. Bassano, Bissolo, Bonifazio, Bordone, Canaletto, Cariani, Giorgione, Licinio, Longhi, Lotto, Palma Vecchio, Polidoro, Savoldo, Schiavone, Tintoretto, Titian.
Hermannstadt. Lotto.
Hopetoun House, N. B. LORD HOPETOUN: Bassano, Beccaruzzi, Canale.
Innsbruck. Rondinelli.
Jesi. LIBRARY: Lotto.
Keir, N. B. MR. ARCHIBALD STIRLING: Beccaruzzi, Bordone, Longhi, Previtali.
Langton, N. B. (near Duns). MRS. BAILLIE-HAMILTON: Polidoro.
Leipzig. Rocco Marconi, Tintoretto.
Lille. Beccaruzzi, Bonifazio, Polidoro, Tintoretto.
Linlathen, N. B. COL. ERSKINE: Bassano, Beccaruzzi, S. del Piombo, Polidoro.
Liverpool. Catena, Rondinelli.
London. NATIONAL GALLERY: Antonello, Bartolommeo Veneto, Basaiti, Bassano, Gentile Bellini, Giovanni Bellini, Bonifazio, Bonsignori, Bordone, Canaletto, Cariani, Capaccio, Catena, Cima, Crivelli, Guardi, Licinio, Pietro Longhi, Lotto, Palma Vecchio, Sebastiano del Piombo, Previtali, Rocco Marconi, Savoldo, Tiepolo, Tintoretto, Titian, Gir. da Treviso, Veronese, Bartolommeo Vivarini.
BURLINGTON HOUSE, DIPLOMA GALLERY: Beccaruzzi.

INDEX OF PLACES. 157

London (*Con.*). SOUTH KENSINGTON MUSEUM, JONES COLLECTION: Crivelli.
LORD ASHBURNHAM: Caprioli, Catena, Rocco Marconi.
LADY ASHBURTON: Crivelli, Licinio, Rondinelli.
APSLEY HOUSE: Beccaruzzi.
LORD BATTERSEA: Polidoro, Tiepolo.
MR. W. B. BEAUMONT: Catena (?).
MR. R. H. BENSON: Bartolommeo Veneto, Basaiti, Bassano, Bissolo, Bonifazio, Caprioli, Cariani, Carpaccio, Catena, Crivelli, S. del Piombo, Polidoro.
MR. F. CAVENDISH-BENTINCK: Longhi.
BRIDGEWATER HOUSE: Bordone, Lotto, Tintoretto, Titian.
LORD BROWNLOW: Bordone, Polidoro, Tintoretto.
MR. C. BUTLER: Basaiti, Bassano, Beccaruzzi, Bonifazio, Catena, Licinio, Montagna, Rocco Marconi, Tintoretto, Bartolommeo Vivarini.
MR. J. P. CARRINGTON: Rocco Marconi.
THE MISSES COHEN: Bordone, Canale, Guardi, Tiepolo, Alvise Vivarini.
MR. MARTIN COLNAGHI: Lotto, Tiepolo.
SIR W. M. CONWAY: Lotto, Tiepolo.
MR. R. CRAWSHAY: Crivelli, Tintoretto.
MR. T. D. CREWS: Bonifazio.
MR. G. DONALDSON: Bassano, Bordone.
DORCHESTER HOUSE: B. Veneto, Beccaruzzi, Canale, Cariani, Guardi, Licinio, Lotto, Polidoro, Rondinelli, Tintoretto.
SIR WM. FARRER: Beccaruzzi, Guardi, Montagna, Polidoro, Tintoretto.
MR. WICKHAM FLOWER: Palma.

INDEX OF PLACES.

London (*Con.*). SIR A. WOLLASTON FRANKS: Guardi.
    SIR JULIAN GOLDSCHMID: Guardi.
    DUKE OF GRAFTON: Caprioli, S. del Piombo.
    HERTFORD HOUSE: Canale, Cima, Crivelli, Guardi.
    MR. J. P. HESELTINE: Catena.
    SIR H. HOWARTH: Previtali, Schiavone.
    LORD HOUGHTON: Guardi.
    MR. ARTHUR JAMES: Guardi, Tintoretto.
    MR. JAMES KNOWLES: Schiavone.
    MARQUIS OF LANSDOWNE: Cariani.
    MR. MUIR MACKENZIE: Polidoro.
    MR. LUDWIG MOND: Giovanni and Gentile Bellini, Bissolo, Canaletto, Catena, Cima, Crivelli, Guardi, P. Longhi, Palma, S. del Piombo, Polidoro, Savoldo, Tintoretto, Titian, Girolamo da Treviso.
    LORD NORTHBROOK: Beccaruzzi, Crivelli, Rocco Marconi.
    DR. J. P. RICHTER: Bonifazio, Bordone, Canale, Guardi, Tiepolo, Veronese.
    LORD ROSEBERY: Bordone, Tintoretto.
    MR. GEORGE SALTING: Basaiti, Cariani, Guardi, Tintoretto, Alvise Vivarini.
    MR. STUART M. SAMUEL: Crivelli.
    SIR B. SAMUELSON: Montagna, Rondinelli.
    SIR MICHAEL SHAW-STEWART: Basaiti, Rocco Marconi.
    MR. J. E. TAYLOR: Cima.
    DUKE OF WESTMINSTER: Canale, Polidoro, Girolamo da Treviso.
    MRS. ANDERSON WESTON: Guardi.
    LORD YARBOROUGH: Polidoro.
Loreto. PALAZZO APOSTOLICO: Lotto.
Lovere. GALLERY TADINI: Jacopo Bellini, Bordone.
Lübeck. Tintoretto.

INDEX OF PLACES. 159

Lucca. GALLERY: Tintoretto.
Lyons. Tintoretto.
Macerata. GALLERY: Crivelli.
Madrid. Giorgione, Lotto, S. del Piombo, Tintoretto, Titian, Veronese.
Maniago. CASA MANIAGO: Titian.
Mantua. ACCADEMIA VIRGILIANA: Bonsignori.
Marseilles. Cariani, Schiavone.
Maser. VILLA BARBARO: Veronese.
Massa Fermana. MUNICIPIO: Crivelli.
Mayence. Tiepolo.
Medole (near Brescia). DUOMO: Titian.
Meiningen. DUCAL PALACE: Basaiti, Bart. Vivarini.
Milan. BRERA: Gentile Bellini, Giovanni Bellini, Bissolo, Bonifazio, Bonsignori, Bordone, Cariani, Carpaccio, Cima, Crivelli, Lotto, Montagna, Palma Vecchio, Previtali, Rondinelli, Savoldo, Tintoretto, Titian, Veronese, Alvise Vivarini.
    POLDI-PEZZOLI: Bonifazio, Cariani, Crivelli, Guardi, Lotto, Montagna, Tiepolo.
    MUSEO CIVICO: Antonello, Beccaruzzi, Cariani, Crivelli, Guardi, Licinio, Lotto, Rondinelli, Schiavone.
    AMBROSIANA: Bartolommeo Veneto, Basaiti, Bassano, Bonifazio, Cariani, Savoldo.
    NATURAL HISTORY MUSEUM: Tiepolo.
    ARCHBISHOP'S PALACE: Licinio.
    BAGATI-VALSECCHI: Gir. da Treviso, Alvise Vivarini.
    BORROMEO: Bartolommeo Veneto, Lotto.
    PALAZZO CHIERICI: Tiepolo.
    SIG. BERTINI: Guardi.
    SIG. B. CRESPI: Bordone, Licinio, Longhi, Savoldo, Tiepolo.
    DR. GUST. FRIZZONI: Giovanni Bellini, Cari-

Milan (*Con.*). ani, Lotto, Montagna, Pordenone, Previtali.
   DUCA MELZI: Bartolommeo Veneto.
   CASA SORMANI: Canaletto.
   PRINCE TRIVULZIO: Antonello, Guardi.
   S. MARIA PRESSO CELSO: Bordone.
Modena. GALLERY: Bassano, Catena, Cima, Licinio, Longhi, Montagna, Polidoro, Alvise Vivarini.
   COUNT LOTARIO RANGONI: Palma.
   S. PIETRO: Girolamo da Treviso.
Monopoli. DUOMO: Gentile Bellini.
Montefiorentino. Alvise Vivarini.
Monte San Giusto. S. MARIA: Lotto
Montpellier. Bassano.
Motta di Livenza. S. MARIA DEI MIRACOLI: Caprioli, Pordenone.
Munich. Basaiti, Bassano, Bordone, Cariani, Cima, Licinio, Lotto, Palma, Polidoro, Rocco Marconi, Schiavone, Tiepolo, Titian.
   LOTZBECK COLLECTION: Bassano, Cariani, Savoldo.
Münster (in W.). Licinio, Gir. da Treviso, Rocco Marconi.
Murano. S. PIETRO: Basaiti, Giovanni Bellini.
   S. MARIA DEGLI ANGELI: Pordenone.
Nancy. Bartolommeo Veneto, Lotto.
Naples. Antonello, Barbari, Giov. Bellini, Lotto, Palma, S. del Piombo, Polidoro, Titian, Alvise Vivarini, Bartolommeo Vivarini.
   MUSEO FILANGIERI: Caprioli, Guardi.
Narbonne. Beccaruzzi.
New Battle, N. B. MARQUIS OF LOTHIAN: Canale, Caprioli, Polidoro, Rocco Marconi.
Newport, U. S. A. MR. T. H. DAVIS: Giov. Bellini, Tintoretto.
New York, U. S. A. METROPOLITAN MUSEUM: Guardi, Tiepolo.

INDEX OF PLACES. 161

New York, U. S. A. (*Con.*). MARQUAND COL. : Savoldo.
            HISTORICAL SOCIETY : Bordone, Cariani.
Nimes.   Catena.
Oldenburg. Beccaruzzi, Cariani, Previtali, Rondinelli.
Olera.   CHURCH : Cima.
Osimo.   MUNICIPIO : Lotto.
Oxford.   TAYLORIAN MUSEUM : Guardi.
           CHRIST CHURCH LIBRARY : Polidoro, Previtali.
Padua.   GALLERY : Basaiti, Beccaruzzi, Jacopo Bellini, Bordone, Catena, Guardi, Licinio, Previtali, Rocco Marconi, Rondinelli, Tiepolo, Alvise Vivarini.
           SANTO : Tiepolo.
           SCUOLA DEL SANTO : Montagna, Titian.
           S. GIUSTINA : Veronese.
           S. MARIA IN VANZO : Bassano, Montagna.
           BISHOP'S PALACE : Montagna.
Panshanger. LORD COWPER : Montagna, Tintoretto.
Paris.   LOUVRE : Antonello, B. Veneto, Bassano, Bonifazio, Bordone, Canale, Cariani, Carpaccio, Catena, Cima, Crivelli, Giorgione, Guardi, Lotto, Montagna, Palma, S. del Piombo, Polidoro, Rondinelli, Schiavone, Tiepolo, Tintoretto, Titian, Veronese, Alvise Vivarini, Bart. Vivarini.
           MME. ANDRÉ : Canale, Catena, Guardi, Polidoro, Tiepolo.
           COUNTESS DE BÉARN : Alvise Vivarini.
           MR. LÉOPOLD GOLDSCHMIDT : Catena, Guardi, Tiepolo.
           M. SALOMON GOLDSCHMIDT : Catena.
           M. MAURICE KANN : Canale.
           M. MARTIN LE ROY : Basaiti.
           M. ALPHONSE DE ROTHSCHILD : S. del Piombo.
           PRINCE SCIARRA : Bonsignori.
Parma.   GALLERY : Beccaruzzi, Cima, S. del Piombo, Schiavone, Tiepolo.

INDEX OF PLACES.

Pausula. S. AGOSTINO: Crivelli.
Peghera. CHURCH: Palma.
Pesaro. GALLERY: Giovanni Bellini.
S. FRANCESCO: Giovanni Bellini.
Piacenza. S. MARIA DELLA CAMPAGNA: Pordenone.
Piove (near Padua). S. NICCOLÒ: Tiepolo.
Ponteranica (near Bergamo). CHURCH: Lotto.
Pordenone. MUNICIPIO: Pordenone.
DUOMO: Pordenone.
Praglia (near Padua). REFECTORY: Montagna.
Ravenna. GALLERY: Rondinelli.
S. DOMENICO: Rondinelli.
Recanati. MUNICIPIO: Lotto.
S. DOMENICO: Lotto.
S. MARIA SOPRA MERCANTI: Lotto.
Richmond. SIR FRANCIS COOK: Bordone, Cima, Crivelli, Guardi, Polidoro, Rocco Marconi, Tiepolo, Tintoretto.
Rimini. MUNICIPIO: Giovanni Bellini.
Rome. VILLA BORGHESE: Antonello, Bassano, Bissolo, Bonifazio, Caprioli, Cariani, Giorgione, Licinio, Lotto, Palma, Polidoro, Savoldo, Titian, Veronese.
CAPITOL: Lotto, Palma, Polidoro, Rondinelli, Savoldo, Tintoretto, Titian.
COLONNA GALLERY: Bonifazio, Bordone, Guardi, Palma, Tintoretto, Gir. da Treviso, Veronese.
CORSINI GALLERY: Bart. Veneto, Bassano, Cariani, Rocco Marconi.
DORIA GALLERY: Bart. Veneto, Basaiti, Beccaruzzi, Bonifazio, Bordone, Catena, Lotto, S. del Piombo, Polidoro, Rondinelli, Tintoretto, Titian.
FARNESINA: S. del Piombo.
LATERAN: Crivelli.

Rome (*Con.*). ROSPIGLIOSI GALLERY : Lotto, Polidoro.
    VATICAN : Cariani, Crivelli, Titian.
    ANTE-CHAMBER TO POPE'S APARTMENTS: Bordone.
    PRINCE CHIGI : Bonifazio, Titian.
    COUNTESS SANTA FIORA : Bassano.
    MISS HERTZ : Licinio,
    DON MARCELLO MASSARENTI : Guardi, Polidoro.
    DONNA LAURA MINGHETTI : Gir. da Treviso.
    SIG. DEL NERO : S. del Piombo.
    S. MARIA DEL POPOLO : S. del Piombo.
    S. PIETRO IN MONTORIO : S. del Piombo.
Rossie Priory, N. B. LORD KINNAIRD : Bassano, Licinio, Tiepolo.
Rouen.   GALLERY : Guardi.
Saletto.   CHURCH : Licinio.
San Daniele (near Udine). DUOMO : Pordenone.
Sedrina.   CHURCH : LOTTO.
Serina.   CHURCH : Palma.
Serravalle. DUOMO: Titian.
    S. ANTONIO : Beccaruzzi.
Seven Oaks. LORD AMHERST : Savoldo.
Siena.   GALLERY : Bordone.
    PALAZZO SARACINI : S. del Piombo.
Spilimbergo. DUOMO : Pordenone.
Strassburg. GALLERY : Basaiti, Beccaruzzi, Bordone, Cariani, Crivelli, Guardi, Montagna, Rocco Marconi, Tiepolo.
Stuttgart. GALLERY : Basaiti, Bassano, Beccaruzzi, Cariani, Carpaccio, Polidoro, Rocco Marconi, Rondinelli.
St. Petersburg. HERMITAGE : Cariani, S. del Piombo.
Susigana. PARISH CHURCH : Pordenone.
Torre (near Pordenone). CHURCH : Pordenone.
Toulouse. Beccaruzzi, Guardi.

INDEX OF PLACES.

Tours.	Bassano, Rocco Marconi.
Trent.	CASTLE, CHAPEL, AND INNER ROOM : Gir. da Treviso.
	4–6 PIAZZA GRANDE, 12 VIA DEL TEATRO : Gir. da Treviso.
Trescorre.	SUARDI CHAPEL : Lotto.
Treviso.	GALLERY : Bordone, Caprioli, Lotto.
	MONTE DI PIETÀ : Beccaruzzi.
	EREDI PERAZZOLO : Beccaruzzi.
	S. ANDREA : Bissolo.
	S. CRISTINA : Lotto.
	DUOMO ; Bissolo, Bordone, Pordenone, Titian.
	S. LUCIA : Beccaruzzi.
	S. NICCOLÒ : Barbari, S. del Piombo, Savoldo.
	18 PIAZZA DEL DUOMO : Barbari.
Turin.	Giovanni Bellini, Guardi, Tiepolo, Tintoretto, B. Vivarini.
Udine.	MUNICIPIO : Tiepolo.
	S. MARIA DELLA PIETÀ : Tiepolo.
Urbino.	DUCAL PALACE : Titian.
	CASA ALBANI : Savoldo.
Venice.	ACADEMY : Antonello, Basaiti, Bassano, Beccaruzzi, Gentile Bellini, Giovanni Bellini, Jacopo Bellini, Bissolo, Bonifazio, Bordone, Cariani, Carpaccio, Catena, Cima, Crivelli, Guardi, Licinio, Longhi, Montagna, Palma Vecchio, Pordenone, Rocco Marconi, Savoldo, Schiavone, Tiepolo, Tintoretto, Titian, Veronese, Alvise Vivarini, Bartolommeo Vivarini.
	MUSEO CORRER : Basaiti, Beccaruzzi, Gentile Bellini, Giovanni Bellini, Jacopo Bellini, Bissolo, Carpaccio, Guardi, Longhi, Rondinelli, Alvise Vivarini.
	PALAZZO DUCALE : Bartolommeo Veneto, Bassano, Giovanni Bellini, Bonsignori, Bordone,

Venice (*Con.*). Carpaccio, Catena, Previtali, Tintoretto, Titian, Veronese.
MANFRIN GALLERY: Beccaruzzi.
QUIRINI-STAMPALIA: Beccaruzzi, Catena, Longhi, Palma, Polidoro, Schiavone, Tiepolo.
PALAZZO REALE: Bassano, Bonifazio, Schiavone, Tintoretto, Titian.
SEMINARIO: Cima, Giorgione, Tiepolo, Alvise Vivarini.
PRINCE GIOVANELLI: Antonello, Basaiti, Bonifazio, Bordone, Catena, Giorgione, Palma, Rocco Marconi, Rondinelli, Tintoretto, Titian.
LADY LAYARD: Barbari, Gentile Bellini, Bissolo, Bonifazio, Bonsignori, Bordone, Carpaccio, Cima, Licinio, Montagna, Palma, S. del Piombo, Previtali, Rondinelli, Savoldo, Alvise Vivarini.
PALAZZO GRASSI: Longhi.
PALAZZO LABIA: Tiepolo.
PALAZZO REZZONICO: Tiepolo.
S. ALVISE: Tiepolo.
SANTI APOSTOLI: Tiepolo.
S. BARTOLOMMEO IN RIALTO: S. del Piombo.
S. BARNABÀ: Veronese.
CARMINE: Cima, Lotto, Schiavone.
SCUOLA DEL CARMINE: Tiepolo.
S. CASSIANO: Rocco Marconi, Tintoretto.
S. CATERINA: Veronese.
S. FANTINO: Rondinelli.
S. FAVA: Tiepolo.
S. FRANCESCO DELLA VIGNA: Giovanni Bellini, Veronese.
FRARI: Barbari, Giovanni Bellini, Licinio, Tiepolo, Titian, Alvise Vivarini, Bartolommeo Vivarini.

Venice (*Con.*). GESUATI: Tiepolo.
GESUITI: Tintoretto, Titian.
S. GIACOMO DELL' ORIO: Bassano, Lotto, Schiavone.
S. GIOBBE: Bordone, Previtali, Savoldo.
S. GIORGIO MAGGIORE: Carpaccio, Tintoretto.
S. GIORGIO DEGLI SCHIAVONI: Carpaccio.
S. GIOVANNI IN BRAGORA: Bissolo, Bordone, Cima, Alvise Vivarini, Bartolommeo Vivarini.
S. GIOVANNI CRISOSTOMO: Giovanni Bellini, S. del Piombo.
S. GIOVANNI ELEMOSINARIO: Pordenone, Titian.
S. GIOVANNI E PAOLO: Bonsignori, Cima, Lotto, Rocco Marconi, Tiepolo, Alvise Vivarini, Bartolommeo Vivarini.
S. GUISEPPE IN CASTELLO: Tintoretto.
S. LIO: Titian.
S. MARCO: Gentile Bellini.
S. MARCUOLO: Titian.
S. MARIA FORMOSA: Palma, Bartolommeo Vivarini.
S. MARIA MATER DOMINI: Bissolo, Catena, Tintoretto.
S. MARIA DELL' ORTO: Beccaruzzi, Giov. Bellini, Cima, Tintoretto.
S. MARIA DELLA PIETÀ: Tiepolo.
S. MARZIALE: Tintoretto, Titian.
S. PAOLO: Tintoretto.
S. PIETRO DI CASTELLO: Basaiti.
REDENTORE: Bissolo, Previtali, Alvise Vivarini.
S. ROCCO: Giorgione, Pordenone, Tintoretto.
SCUOLA DI S. ROCCO: Tintoretto, Titian.
SALUTE: Basaiti, Polidoro, Tintoretto, Titian, Girolamo da Treviso.
S. SALVATORE: Titian.

INDEX OF PLACES. 167

Venice (*Con.*). SCALZI : Tiepolo.
S. SEBASTIANO : Titian, Veronese.
S. SIMEON PROFETA : Catena.
S. STEFANO : Pordenone, Tintoretto.
S. TROVASO : Jacopo Bellini, Catena, Tintoretto.
S. VITALE : Carpaccio.
S. ZACCARIA : Giovanni Bellini, Tintoretto.

Verona. GALLERY : Bart. Veneto, Basaiti, Bassano, Giovanni Bellini, Jacopo Bellini, Crivelli, Guardi, Montagna, Polidoro, Previtali, Tiepolo, Titian, Gir. da Treviso, Veronese.
DUOMO : Titian.
S. GIORGIO : Veronese.
S. NAZARO E CELSO : Montagna.
S. PAOLO : Veronese.

Vicenza. GALLERY : Antonello, Bassano, Cariani, Cima, Montagna, Tiepolo, Tintoretto, Veronese.
PALAZZO LOSCHI : Bassano, Giorgione.
VILLA VALMARANA : Tiepolo.
S. CORONA : Giovanni Bellini, Montagna.
DUOMO : Montagna.
S. LORENZO : Montagna.
MONTE BERICO : Montagna, Veronese.
S. STEFANO : Palma.

Vienna. IMPERIAL MUSEUM : Barbari, Basaiti, Bassano, Beccaruzzi, Bissolo, Bonifazio, Bordone, Caprioli, Cariani, Carpaccio, Catena, Cima, Giorgione, Licinio, Lotto, Palma, S. del Piombo, Polidoro, Previtali, Savoldo, Schiavone, Tintoretto, Titian, Gir. da Treviso, Veronese, Alvise Vivarini, Bartolommeo Vivarini.
ACADEMY : Bassano, Beccaruzzi, Caprioli, Cariani, Polidoro, Schiavone, Tiepolo, Tintoretto, Alvise Vivarini.

Vienna (Con.). CZERNIN : Bordone, Rocco Marconi, Titian.
        HARRACH COLLECTION : Basaiti, Licinio, Polidoro.
        LICHTENSTEIN : Canale, Palma Vecchio, Savoldo.
Viterbo. MUNICIPIO : S. del Piombo.
Weimar. GALLERY : Barbari.
Windsor Castle. Canale, Caprioli, Alvise Vivarini.
Woburn Abbey. Bassano, Canale, Tintoretto,
Würzburg. ARCHBISHOP'S PALACE : Tiepolo.
Zogno. CHURCH : Cariani.

A Selection from the
Catalogue of

G. P. PUTNAM'S SONS

Complete Catalogues sent
on application

Works on the Italian Renaissance

By Bernhard Berenson

The Venetian Painters of the Renaissance

With an essay on their genius and an Index to the Works of the Principal Venetian Painters. Frontispiece. *Third Edition*, revised and enlarged. Crown 8°. Gilt top.

"One of the best things I have ever read on so delicate a subject. It merits translating into Italian."—SIGNOR BONCHI, writing in *La Cultura*.

"A genuine contribution to the literature of art."—*Boston Transcript*.

The Florentine Painters of the Renaissance

With an essay on their genius and an Index to the Works of the Principal Florentine Painters. Frontispiece. *Third Revised and Enlarged Edition*. Crown 8°.

"A highly competent student of Italian Art; a practitioner of the most modern methods of investigation."—*London Times*.

The Central Italian Painters of the Renaissance

With an essay on their genius and an Index to the Works of the Principal Central Italian Painters. Frontispiece. *Second Revised and Enlarged Edition*. Crown 8°.

"A scholarly and artistic discussion of decoration and illustration, followed by brief critiques on the different artists of Central Italy. The last 75 pages contain an invaluable index. The index alone is worth far more than the price of the book."—*Wooster Post-Graduate*.

The North Italian Painters of the Renaissance

With an essay on their genius and an Index to the Works of the Principal North Italian Painters. Crown 8°. Frontispiece.

"This little book is written by a man who knows his subject well and who is thoroughly in sympathy with the spirit of the Renaissance."

(*Send for descriptive circular of books on art.*)

New York   **G. P. Putnam's Sons**   London

A Work of First Importance

The History of Painting
From the Fourth to the Early Nineteenth Century

By Richard Muther, Ph.D.
Professor in the University of Breslau; author of
"History of Modern Painting," etc.

Translated from the German and edited with critical notes by

George Kriehn, Ph.D.
Sometime Instructor in the Johns Hopkins University and Assistant Professor in the Leland Stanford Jr. University

Richard Muther is a critic of art at once brilliant and sound, whose reputation is now world-wide. Muther's work is not an art history of the hackneyed kind that follows the chronicles of painting into its obscure and insignificant ramifications, and weighs down the narrative with masses of biographical and descriptive data. The aim of the present book is, while not neglecting technical questions, to interpret the great masterpieces of painting as human documents and manifestations of the dominant feelings and tendencies of the epochs to which they belong.

2 Volumes, 8vo, with 85 Illustrations.

Send for descriptive circular

G. P. PUTNAM'S SONS
New York   London

"*Supplies a genuine need.*"—*N. Y. Observer*

Sacred Symbols in Art

By Elizabeth E. Goldsmith

8vo. 53 Illustrations.

"Symbolism underlies so much of the art of the past that the one who visits the art galleries without some knowledge of it is like a wanderer in a labyrinth who has not the key. And even for those who have a fair knowledge of the common symbols a ready-reference book is invaluable. Any one who has had the experience of looking through a half-dozen books in search of some particular thing, will be glad to find a book like this with its double index and cross references. In brief, it is an excellent book of reference, useful alike to the traveller and the student."—*Boston Eve. Transcript.*

"The information is compact, concise; the illustrations are frequent and beautifully reproduced. It can be especially recommended to those who intend to visit European art museums."—*Review of Reviews.*

G. P. Putnam's Sons
New York   London

www.ingramcontent.com/pod-product-compliance
Lightning Source LLC
Chambersburg PA
CBHW032138160426
43197CB00008B/697